THE FINANCIAL FOUR

The Plan for Living Abundantly, Giving Outrageously, and Winning the Game of Wealth

MARK A. AHO

with Kirsten D. Samuel

Also by Mark A. Aho

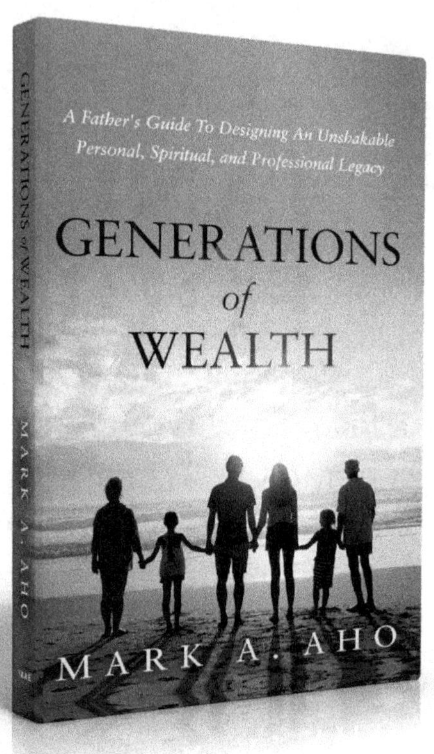

Your legacy tomorrow will be determined by how you live today.

No one wants to *just get by.* The truth is you can design an unshakeable personal, spiritual, and professional legacy that you pass on for generations to come. Discover the proven process for creating a rich legacy that outlives you.

THE FINANCIAL FOUR

The Plan for Living Abundantly, Giving Outrageously, and Winning the Game of Wealth

MARK A. AHO

with Kirsten D. Samuel

THE FINANCIAL FOUR

Published by ethos collective
P.O. Box 43
Powell, OH 43065
Ethoscollective.vip

Library of Congress Cataloguing:
Softcover: 978-1-63680-067-7
Hardcover: 978-1-63680-068-4
E-book: 978-1-63680-069-1

Available in hardcover, softcover, e-book, and audiobook

DEDICATION

This book is dedicated to my parents, Arne and June Aho,
and my wife Julie's parents, Pinky and Merle Schiavo.
I learned how to be a family steward from them.
These four people mean the world to me,
and I love them dearly.

CONTENTS

FOREWORD

A knock on the door more than thirty years ago introduced us to Mark Aho.

Soon we were taking investment classes from him at Northern Michigan University, and he became our financial advisor. Kris's father had recently passed away, and her mother, who suffered from memory loss, lived alone on the family farm. The thought of being responsible for someone else's finances was daunting.

Our original goals as her mother's caretakers were

1. Providing for Kris's mother's care.
2. Keeping and managing the farm.
3. Being good stewards for Kris's sisters and their families.

Fear can lead to procrastination, indecision, and missed opportunities. Missed opportunities can cause one to fall short of one's goals. It's difficult to be wise and well informed about all aspects of life, which is why competent and wise advisors are essential. We overcame our fears and procrastination, which allowed us to be good stewards of Kris's mother's savings. We took care of her mom's needs, kept and managed the family farm, and had some savings left over for Kris and her siblings. Kris's parents had a strong work ethic, lived frugally, and believed in saving and investing wisely. They would have been pleased to know that their years of hard work, saving, and investing enabled them to remain independent in their declining years, to provide something for their family, and to keep the farm that had been such a big part of their lives.

Since the first meeting thirty years ago, we established clear goals, a plan to achieve those milestones, and implemented our planning. This has made a tremendous difference in our lives.

My parents also believed in hard work, frugality, consistent saving, and investing. My dad's salary at Detroit Edison was modest, but providing for and supporting his family was very important to him. Soon after returning home from the service following World War II, he joined an investment club. Dad put twenty-five dollars into a fund at each monthly meeting, which the club then invested in stocks.

When my parents retired, they depended upon their two meager pensions and social security for income. They had paid off their mortgage and accumulated savings from years of slow and steady investment in stocks. When Dad resided in assisted living and Mom was in a memory care unit, they were able to support themselves financially. Having clearly set goals, taking advantage of opportunities to invest on a regular basis, and being frugal, allowed them to live the life they wanted after retirement, knowing they could be financially independent.

After becoming grandparents, my folks wanted to provide each grandchild with a financial legacy. Each newborn grandchild received one hundred dollars of Detroit Edison stock with an automatic reinvestment plan. We kept and carefully managed our children's gifted nest eggs. When our daughter started a business, her grandparents' gift had increased in value to more than twenty thousand dollars. This helped her start her business. My parents' gift of $100 of stock grew to be a down payment of over twenty thousand dollars for our son's first house. Dad loved getting updates on the growth of his gifts, knowing he had made a difference in his grandchildren's lives.

Most of us have little knowledge or background in investing. Because of this we hesitate, fearing the loss of our savings. But we don't have to allow fear or ignorance to keep us from reaching our financial dreams and goals. We can seek out the help and information we need. Mark's new book, *The Financial Four*, helps provide the answers to four of life's most critical questions:

1. Will my family be all right?
2. Will my family and I be able to live the life we want after retirement?
3. Can I afford to be generous to others?
4. Have I done enough?

His book provides the structure and perspective to make smart decisions and progress towards reaching your goals.

Kris and I are thankful we answered the door when Mark knocked. Reading his new book will give you the tools and knowledge to better your life too.

—Dr. Donn G (Bud) Kipka Jr., DDS

NOTE TO THE READER

Thank you for spending some of your valuable time reading this book. The goal of *The Financial Four* is to get you started or restarted on the right track toward fully living your life while also achieving your most desired life goals. Everyone, especially family stewards, desires to answer life's four questions:

1. Will my family be all right?
2. Will my family and I be able to live the life we want after retirement?
3. Can I afford to be generous to others?
4. Have I done enough?

To ensure your financial and life success, you must take these questions in order and be able to answer "yes" to each one before moving on to the next. If you can do that on your own, great! If not, it would be worth your while to hire a competent financial advisor to help get a plan of action in place. Yes, an advisor will charge you a fee; however, with the right financial advisor, your outcome will most likely far outweigh any fee you pay.

As you seek out an advisor, I encourage you to choose wisely. Like all things in life, there are differences amongst advisors. Take the time to find one who is a good fit for you. Ask about their niche client. My firm's niche client, for example, is the family steward. These clients usually spend less than they earn and are interested in finding successful answers to the financial four questions. They want to make wise decisions that will empower them to leave a legacy for those they love.

Whatever your goals are for your finances, you want to choose a financial advisor who is focused on helping you achieve them.

I hope this book will encourage you to take steps toward your goals.

God bless you always,
Mark A. Aho

PART 1

PRE-GAME ANALYSIS

INTRODUCTION

John Grey doesn't think he's anything special. He's a typical guy who keeps his head down, works hard, loves his wife and family, and helps others.

John is a regular at his local high school's football games. The kids at the school call him Pops, a term of respect. They all know him well because he volunteers at the games and other school events. John loves talking with the students, learning about their interests, encouraging them in their studies, and most importantly, dreaming with them. He says it keeps him young.

John and his wife, Sandy, are considering selling their home of 30 years where they raised their kids. While they love that home, John and Sandy know it is time to bless another family with the place where they built treasured memories. They joke about rattling around in it these days. Each room contains memories and echoes of their children who now have their own families. As they discuss what selling their home means to them, several questions arise about their next steps. Where would they like to live? What type of home would suit their needs moving forward? Is now the right time or should they wait a few more years? Have they adequately prepared for the next phase of life? What about their children and grandchildren?

They have dreams they would like to pursue but feel unsure what step to take next. Life feels strangely uncertain.

⁂

Most people want answers to four questions that affect their financial future and legacy.

1. Will I have enough?
2. Can I live the life I want to live?
3. Can I help my kids, grandkids, family members, and others?
4. Did I do enough?

Each of these questions deals with core issues related to the biblical concept of abundance. In the Old Testament in Deuteronomy 28, God told the people of Israel that obedience to Him came with blessings, which included prosperity. As God's followers, He instructs us to steward all of life well. I call this being a family steward. When we follow God's commands, He provides everything we need to care for ourselves, our family, and others. As we work through each question, we will also address the core principle of biblical abundance.

Spoiler alert: The answer to each question is *Yes*! You can experience abundance as you work through each question. Using John and Sandy as our test couple, we'll journey through the steps and learn how to use biblical principles and practical application to live well and give with abundance.

We'll start with a pregame analysis. Every good coach reviews past experiences, sets a goal, then gathers the team to talk through the anticipated game plan.

Are you ready?

At the end of each chapter, I'll ask you to take a new action step toward achieving your dream. Don't skip over this part. Instead, grab a notebook, or use the space provided in this book to write out your next best action step based on that chapter's content.

Achieve Your Dream—Action Step

Answer the four questions in this chapter based on what you see today:

Will I have enough?

Can I live the life I want to live?

Can I help my kids, grandkids, family members, and others?

Did I do enough?

1
WHAT DOES IT MEAN TO BE A FAMILY STEWARD?

This is the great paradox of living the blessed life: when we give without thought to whether or not we will receive, then we receive.

—Robert Morris

Family steward. It sounds like an old-fashioned term, and it may be, but I can't think of a better description for this person. You've met them. Perhaps you are one.

The family steward rarely stands out like a celebrity. This person could be the husband or wife, married or single, or the husband and wife may work together to achieve their family's goals. Not drawn to notoriety, they work hard to provide for their family. Quietly, they walk through every day with deeply held beliefs. Often these beliefs come from their parents and grandparents. Therefore, it's difficult to change their minds. They've wrestled through their personal, religious, business, and financial convictions and won't be swayed without tremendous proof.

Generally conservative in the way they think, the family steward chooses a quiet lifestyle that matches their beliefs.

They tend to stay more mainstream than follow the latest fad or progressive point of view. Family matters to them, not just in nodding assent, but in the core of their being. Being called a family man or family woman is a badge of honor worn proudly.

FAMILY STEWARD EXAMPLE—JOHN AND SANDY GREY

John and Sandy Grey exemplify the family steward. With their strong faith in God, they look at life through a lens of gratitude. John and Sandy regard each other, their children, and grandchildren as gifts from God. From their wedding day, John and Sandy have filtered every decision and expenditure through this lens, considering how each choice would benefit their family in the present as well as the future.

To look at John and Sandy today, you'd think they held high-paying jobs, which isn't necessarily true. One thing that defines family stewards is their decision to save something from every income source. Living comfortably, but without spending everything they earned, slowly over time, the Greys built their savings account. Often, they learned how to fix something themselves, partly because it was a challenge but also to save some money. In the early years of their marriage, they lived off John's income and saved Sandy's to build up a reserve.

John and Sandy grew up near the Chicago area. They went to school together, were high school sweethearts, and married a few years after graduating from college. When he was a child, John's family had a cottage on a small, sandy-bottomed lake outside of the Marquette area in the Upper Peninsula of Michigan. He had fond memories of spending summers in the Upper Peninsula of Michigan, catching fish, swimming, and sitting by a warm campfire cooking s'mores in the evening.

Interestingly, while John's mom and dad taught him well how to budget and manage his money, Sandy grew up with a single mom. She never learned to save because they always had barely enough. Sandy watched the hours her mom worked to provide for her and her two brothers. While Sandy's mom lived within her means, she couldn't save much beyond that. When John and Sandy decided to marry, they discussed how they would handle their money. Sandy knew what it felt like to live on the edge of survival and she wanted more from their life. They spent hours discussing their dreams and desires for their family.

Both respect their parents, who taught them the value of hard work. John and Sandy lived frugally even after they became well established in their careers. They knew they would have to be good savers to reach some of their goals. With their goals in mind, John and Sandy sought out relationships with people who seemed to manage their money well. They believed it was important to care for their present needs while planning for their family's future, so they made a point of listening and learning about finances from those who were a little further along in life. Then John and Sandy applied what they learned a little bit at a time.

Money became a frequent topic of conversation and source of conflict due to their diverse family backgrounds. Sandy wanted to enjoy their extra combined resources but also felt fearful when their bank account dropped below a certain threshold. For Sandy, money in the bank signified a secure future. John preferred living on a pre-determined budget. He had no problem setting aside money for vacations and a few meals out a month, but he wasn't spontaneous with financial decisions. When Sandy came home from a shopping trip with more than what she intended to purchase, John often had a few choice words. Because Sandy also worked full time, she felt entitled to spend a little extra now and then. Together, they struggled to find a balance.

When John looks back, he wonders about the time they bought their first home after their first child was born. Both knew it was more than they could afford, but they wanted it, and the bank approved the loan. John had run the numbers multiple times and figured if they lived frugally they'd manage the new mortgage payment on top of their other monthly bills. After a few months in the house, however, they regretted their decision. They had sought good counsel but realized that living at the end of their budget brought unnecessary anxiety. For a while, Sandy worked part time to ease the financial strain. While it wasn't the best decision for them, after paying childcare, it helped a bit. Eventually, John picked up a part-time gig that paid well and provided the additional needed relief.

Not only did the decision to buy that first house cause a strain on their finances, it stretched their faith. Because they believe in God, Jesus Christ, and the Bible, John and Sandy sought to serve God first. By working the extra hours to keep current with their bills, John and Sandy felt the strain in the marriage and in their spiritual relationship. After a year or so struggling to survive, they chose to sell their house and find something more affordable.

Family Stewards Make Difficult Decisions

Family stewards make difficult decisions, like downsizing to a smaller mortgage payment, because the question that they must answer first is, "Can I provide for my family?" Rather than go into a large amount of debt, the family steward often delays purchasing certain items until they either have the money saved or are in a better financial position. They understand and live with the tension of desires and delayed gratification. Their first concern focuses on taking care of their family. Do the children have adequate clothing and shoes? Can they put nutritious food on the table? The family steward may even learn to garden, take a plumbing course, or pick up an odd job here and there to provide extra income. To the family steward, people matter more than the accumulation of things.

In *Generations of Wealth*, my first book, I relay my early struggles to provide for my family and learn how to be a family steward. I made plenty of mistakes along the way. But, thankfully, I listened and learned from others how to manage my time and resources, including my finances, in a more healthy and biblically-minded manner. Some of my tough decisions involved driving an older model car, living in a smaller home for a short time, and using the home repair skills my dad taught me to save money on repair costs. These family steward lessons deepened my faith in the future and my entrepreneurial spirit. I believed then as I do now that anything is possible with hard work and stewarding resources well.

Family Stewards Prioritize Financial Independence

Family stewards recognize that providing for their families means not being dependent on anyone, including the government. Like John and Sandy, the family steward works to become financially independent. Through consistent saving, the family steward builds wealth over time. They don't rely on a large windfall. Rather they understand how compounding interest and regular contributions steadily grow the financial reserves. They long for the day when they have enough to help others who experience sudden or unforeseen crises.

Some of the most valuable resources a family steward passes on to their children and grandchildren are not financial. Stewardship of relationships, faith, and a positive mindset set their families up to succeed just as much as a large bank account.

Busy working and raising their children, family stewards recognize they need help and wise counsel regarding their money. Like most people, they may not fully understand the financial markets or how to maximize the growth potential of their savings and investments. They have worked hard and understand that a financial advisor can affirm their progress and guide them as they create a solid plan for the future.

To the family steward, anything less than providing well means failure. Some stewards, like John, invest time to learn and understand financial planning. But he needed confirmation that he'd done a good job to this point.

ACHIEVE YOUR DREAM—ACTION STEP

God entrusts our families to us as gifts to be treasured and cared for. We honor God and them by doing all we can to provide for our loved ones now while preparing for a secure future. What does the term family steward mean to you?

2
THE FOUR CORE PRINCIPLES FOR SUCCESS

If you don't know where you are going, any road can take you there.

—Lewis Carroll

At various points in life, most of us will ask the same four questions:

1. Will my family and I be okay?
2. Will my family and I be able to live the life we want?
3. Can I be generous to others?
4. Have I done enough?

To the family steward, answering these questions in the affirmative provides proof of their success. It's important to note that while wealth is part of the success equation, the answers aren't measured exclusively in financial terms. A fulfilling and successful life is measured by all aspects of life—relationships, benevolence, career, faith, physical and mental health—which is why so many of us approach our later years of life questioning our decisions and actions.

So often when I talk with people about leaving a legacy, they immediately steer the conversation to the amount of money they'll leave to their heirs. I remind them that while finances are an important aspect of legacy, the greatest aspect of legacy relates to the wisdom, beliefs, and attitudes passed along to future generations.

Let me give you an example. My parents instilled four core lessons into me and my siblings: hard work, faith, belief in the future, and an entrepreneurial spirit. These four lessons formed a lasting legacy in my life. And not only my life but also in the lives of my two children because I've passed those same lessons on to them.

I explain these core lessons in greater detail in my book, *Generations of Wealth: A Father's Guide To Designing An Unshakable Personal, Spiritual, and Professional Legacy*, but I want to give you an overview here.

LESSON #1: HARD WORK

My mother and father worked hard throughout their lives. As an entrepreneurial endeavor, Dad and Mom owned and operated some motel-style cabins. Dad spent his off hours either building or fixing something for that business.

Monday through Friday, from 7:00 a.m. to 3:00 p.m., Dad worked his day job at the copper mine. He arrived home around 3:30 p.m., had dinner, and took a twenty-minute nap. Then, Dad and I worked on the cabins.

I didn't think much about it at the time, but when I reflect on those days of helping my dad, I realize how fortunate I was to have spent that time with him. In retrospect, I learned everything I needed to know about owning a house too. I can install a new light or rewire a fixture in a home, replace the roof, and everything in between.

Mom worked hard, too, using a different skill set. Whereas my dad was introverted and put his energy into physical projects, my extroverted mom made everyone feel welcome. She warmly greeted guests and helped them find their cabins. She loved the hospitality involved with their business and was very good at it, too, which rubbed off on me.

In a way, I got the best of both worlds when it came to learning about hard work. My dad taught me about physical labor and how to build things. My mom taught me about people, which is also a valuable skill.

LESSON #2: FAITH

My dad was a non-practicing Apostolic Lutheran, and my mom was a Roman Catholic. She took me to church every Sunday while my dad—you guessed it—worked. Mom's involvement in the church significantly influenced the establishing and maintaining of my faith.

But, as is true for every person, I had to make my relationship with God my own. I spend time daily reading the Bible, talking with God, and learning to apply what I learn from the Bible and studying the teachings of Jesus. I've learned to love and care for people, to live generously, and to be intentional both in word and actions. Therefore, I hold tightly to my faith and belief. These values and life bedrocks play a key role in who I am, how I treat people, how I approach life, and what I do every day. God's love and what He has done for humanity anchors me, and that's never going to change.

LESSON #3: BELIEF IN THE FUTURE

The way I see it, you can choose to live optimistically positive or pessimistically negative. I choose to live with optimism because my faith extends to a belief in the future of humanity's ability to make the world a better place. That means I keep my focus on what lies ahead.

Regretting or dwelling on a mistake is neither healthy nor productive. Expending energy to wish away the negative actions of the past is not only a waste of time but it also limits your ability to contribute to a better future.

Lack of faith can cloud your financial decision-making as well as your life choices. I've had many clients tell me they think there's nothing left out there to invest in, that all the good ideas are taken. That line of thinking is categorically incorrect. There's so much good in the world and many reasons to believe in the future. I love getting the opportunity to help clients develop a mindset that enables growth and fosters prosperity.

What do you allow to influence your view of the future? If you continually feed your heart and mind with negative news, you will lose faith in the future. I suggest you find positive influences. Stop dwelling on the past. Focus on the present moment and what you can control and have faith in the future.

Lesson #4: Entrepreneurial Spirit

My parents instilled the importance of an entrepreneurial spirit in me at a young age. I saw how hard they worked at multiple jobs to make ends meet. Their example taught me the importance of saving. And what I learned from them gave me an advantage in my career and my personal life.

By the time I was in high school, I managed my parents' finances. While that may sound strange, I learned valuable lessons about budgeting, banking processes, and business management. I learned that it's okay to try something new, take a calculated risk, make adjustments along the way, fix what's broken, and keep moving forward. This mindset continues to influence my professional and personal decisions.

If you are married to someone with an entrepreneurial spirit, your spouse needs your belief in them and their integrity.

Tough times will come. Entrepreneurialism doesn't involve one success after another. Failure is a big part of success. How entrepreneurs learn from and respond to failure plays a significant role in determining their ultimate success. To respond favorably—with hope and wisdom—entrepreneurs need the support of their significant other to persevere.

Stop for a moment and assess where you are right now. Don't judge; simply evaluate your current status in all areas of life. This holistic approach helps you look *forward* with clarity. Your present reality is the aggregate of every decision you've made up until now. To answer those four questions accurately, you must evaluate your reality. Again, this isn't a time to judge or be critical; it just is.

The Faithful Steward

The following story from the Bible offers a glimpse at what it means to be a faithful steward. Read on as Jesus tells his disciples the story of the faithful and unfaithful stewards.

> "Again, it will be like a man going on a journey, who called his servants and entrusted his wealth to them. To one he gave five bags of gold, to another two bags, and to another one bag, each according to his ability. Then he went on his journey. The man who had received five bags of gold went at once and put his money to work and gained five bags more. So also, the one with two bags of gold gained two more. But the man who had received one bag went off, dug a hole in the ground and hid his master's money.
>
> "After a long time the master of those servants returned and settled accounts with them. The man who had received five bags of gold brought the other five. 'Master,' he said, 'you entrusted me with five bags of gold. See, I have gained five more.'
>
> "His master replied, 'Well done, good and faithful servant! You have been faithful with a few things; I will

put you in charge of many things. Come and share your master's happiness!'

"The man with two bags of gold also came. 'Master,' he said, 'you entrusted me with two bags of gold; see, I have gained two more.'

"His master replied, 'Well done, good and faithful servant! You have been faithful with a few things; I will put you in charge of many things. Come and share your master's happiness!'

"Then the man who had received one bag of gold came. 'Master,' he said, 'I knew that you are a hard man, harvesting where you have not sown and gathering where you have not scattered seed. So I was afraid and went out and hid your gold in the ground. See, here is what belongs to you.'

"His master replied, 'You wicked, lazy servant! So you knew that I harvest where I have not sown and gather where I have not scattered seed? Well then, you should have put my money on deposit with the bankers, so that when I returned I would have received it back with interest.

"'So take the bag of gold from him and give it to the one who has ten bags. For whoever has will be given more, and they will have an abundance. Whoever does not have, even what they have will be taken from them. And throw that worthless servant outside, into the darkness, where there will be weeping and gnashing of teeth.'"

—Matthew 25:14–30 (NIV)

Often Jesus taught key lessons through stories or parables. In this parable, the faithful steward took what he was given and invested it wisely. The faithful steward exhibited an abundance mindset. He learned well from the Master to take calculated risks with faith in the future. The Master commended this steward for his faithful work and investments. It's a story that exemplifies the biblical concept of abundance.

WHAT IS BIBLICAL ABUNDANCE?

Whether they acknowledge it or not, people experience life with either an *abundance mindset* or a *scarcity mindset.* Stephen Covey coined these terms in his bestselling book, *The 7 Habits of Highly Effective People.* The abundance mindset[1] says there is more than enough money, food, love, and opportunity for everyone. The abundance mindset creates excitement, confidence, and faith in life. When you live with this mindset, you sense hope flowing around you in every aspect of your life. You believe the future is full of possibility.

I prefer the abundance mindset to the scarcity mindset because of the hope it offers. I also believe it is biblical. Consider the two following examples of abundance in the Bible. The first shows up in all four gospels, as we read about Jesus feeding of the 5,000 (Matthew 14:13–21, Mark 6:30–44, Luke 9:10–17, and John 6:1–15). Jesus fed five thousand men (plus women and children) with a boy's lunch—five rolls and two fish. What a miracle! But notice the abundance in this story.

> When they had all had enough to eat, he said to his disciples, "Gather the pieces that are left over. Let nothing be wasted." So they gathered them and filled twelve baskets with the pieces of the five barley loaves left over by those who had eaten.
>
> —John 6 12–13 (NIV)

When the disciples collected the remaining food, there were *twelve baskets* of leftovers. Not only did Jesus feed everyone, He supplied more than enough—in abundance. No one left that meal hungry.

Jesus's first recorded miracle showed His mother's faith and offers another example of His generous and gracious abundance. Mary heard the wine had run out during a wedding party she was attending. That wasn't good for the host, in fact, it surely meant being publicly disgraced. Mary went to Jesus and asked Him to solve the problem. She exhibits her faith by telling the servants to do whatever He asked them to do. The servants followed Jesus's instructions to fill six, thirty-gallon jars with water. They did, and then served a drink to the host. The abundance in this story comes not only from the fact that Jesus turned water into enough wine to serve the wedding party but also in that the wine was good—even *better* than what the host had served up to that point.

I live by this passage in 2 Corinthians 9:6–11 (NLT):

> Remember this—a farmer who plants only a few seeds will get a small crop. But the one who plants generously will get a generous crop. You must each decide in your heart how much to give. And don't give reluctantly or in response to pressure. "For God loves a person who gives cheerfully." And God will generously provide all you need. Then you will always have everything you need and plenty left over to share with others. As the Scriptures say,
>
> "They share freely and give generously to the poor. Their good deeds will be remembered forever."
>
> For God is the one who provides seed for the farmer and then bread to eat. In the same way, he will provide and increase your resources and then produce a great harvest of generosity in you.
>
> Yes, you will be enriched in every way so that you can always be generous. And when we take your gifts to those who need them, they will thank God.

God gives generously, abundantly, to us when we ask Him, follow His ways, and submit to His will. I'm not talking about "name it and claim it" theology. This abundance mindset views all of life as *more*. It's having faith in the future because the past provides evidence of God's provision.

The abundance mindset takes what you learn and understand and uses that to move forward into the next endeavor.

Examining the Scarcity Mindset

A scarcity mindset sets limits and restrictions on *everything*. Consider the maxim, "The early bird gets the worm." Scarcity thinking says there's only one worm. Whoever gets it that day eats. If you're late or someone gets there before you, you starve.

According to Covey[2], people with the scarcity mindset "see life as having only so much, as though there were only one pie out there. And if someone were to get a big piece of the pie, it would mean less for everybody else. The Scarcity Mentality is the zero-sum paradigm of life."

Stanford psychologist, Carol Dweck, studied students' mindsets and found a significant difference in the learning capacity between those with a growth (abundance) mindset and those with a fixed (scarcity) mindset. Those with a growth mindset believed intelligence could be developed to overcome academic challenges. Those with a fixed mindset believed their intelligence level was predetermined and they could not change it. In her book, *Mindset: The New Psychology of Success*, Dweck provides her research and analysis about the effects of growth and fixed mindsets. "In the fixed mindset, everything is about the outcome. If you fail—or if you're not the best—it's all been wasted. The growth mindset allows people to value what they're doing *regardless of the outcome*. They're tackling problems, charting new courses, working on important issues. Maybe they haven't found the cure for cancer, but the search was deeply meaningful."[3]

The unfaithful steward exhibits a scarcity mindset. He took what he was given and buried it out of fear of potential future problems. The master condemned him for being wicked and lazy. Living with a scarcity mindset focuses on fear and lack. You never have enough and envy anyone you perceive has more than you. That's not a way to live.

Develop an Abundance Mindset for the Long Game

When it comes to investing wisely, the abundance mindset guides you into the long game. And as a financial planner, my goal is to help you understand the long-term aspect of being an investor. Why? Because if you can't understand that a wise investor plays a long game, not a short game, you aren't an investor.

With an abundance mindset as an investor, you choose your investments wisely, based on historical data, and then believe in their continued upward trend. Yes, dips and dives come, but you don't panic. You patiently wait and watch, confident that the final outcome will be more. That attitude puts you on the path to being a faithful steward.

The faithful steward exemplifies the attitude of an investor and the parable illustrates the first three investment principles every investor needs to acknowledge and adopt. I explained these in detail in *Generations of Wealth: A Father's Guide to Designing an Unshakable Personal, Spiritual, and Professional Legacy*. Here they are briefly explained:

1. **Trust**—Have unrelenting faith in the future of our planet, humanity, and your success.
2. **Patience**—Understand that your investments will fluctuate, but over time, your investments will increase. Patient people are peaceful.
3. **Discipline**—Accept that financial success takes hard work and frugality. You say yes to moderation and no to excess.

Merriam-Webster defines *invest*[4] as: to commit (money) in order to earn a financial return; to make use of for future benefits or advantages. I want to highlight a couple key phrases in this definition.

First, *to commit.* A person must make a conscious, deliberate choice to invest a defined portion of their income for future profit. If you aren't willing to set a percentage of your income aside for future use, then you can't be an investor. The wisest stewards decide how best to use their funds, talents, and giftings to impact their future.

Second, *future benefit or advantage.* In our current society, we've lost much of the desire to look beyond today. As Dave Ramsey says, "It is human nature to want it and want it now; it is also a sign of immaturity. Being willing to delay pleasure for a greater result is a sign of maturity." While I understand that we aren't guaranteed one more day of life, choosing to spend every dollar you make today is short-sighted.

Imagine a husband refusing to purchase life insurance to provide some stability for his family in the event of his untimely death. That's short-sighted, narrow-minded, and irresponsible in my opinion. That is the foolish steward burying his money in the ground. A person who cannot discipline himself or herself to put a small percentage of income into investments for the future is not an investor.

To be an investor, you must be willing to assume a level of risk, have faith in the future, and exhibit patient understanding that your investments will grow over time. You don't focus on the short-term rise and fall of your investment portfolio. Rather, you look at your various investments over five years and longer. An investor cares more about the historical trends of their investments and the future potential than they do about the regular market fluctuations.

Let's look again at the four questions we started this chapter with:

1. Will my family and I be okay?
2. Will my family and I be able to live the life we want?
3. Can I be generous to others?
4. Have I done enough?

If you and I sat across the table sipping coffee, how would you answer those questions? Which one troubles you the most at this point in your life? Do you wonder if you've passed on your values, financial beliefs, and spiritual beliefs to you children? As a family steward, I hope your focus is first on making sure your children catch and live out your positive beliefs. Yes, you want to be able to provide for them financially now and in the future, but remember that an essential aspect of success is that your children become productive, God-fearing, active members of society who think for themselves.

Eventually, you will answer each question. The goal I have for every client is that he or she is able to answer these questions with a resounding, "Yes!" When you, as your family's steward, can answer these questions positively, you will know that your hard work and sacrifice was worth the effort.

As you read through this book, keep these questions forefront. It's not enough to assume you will answer the question the way you desire; you must have a plan. Before you stop reading, let's talk about what this plan might look like.

❧ ❧ ❧ ❧ ❧

John and Sandy, now in their mid to late fifties, wonder if they're on the right track. Sandy went back to a full-time job once the kids were out of grade school. Smart with their money, they minimized their debt and maximized their 401(k) plans and built a decent-sized stock portfolio outside of their retirement accounts. They made the decision years ago to pay down their mortgage quickly, buy cars they could easily either pay for outright or pay off with a small loan, and carry no credit card debt.

At this point in their lives, their burning question is, "Will we leave the legacy we desire?" John and Sandy know they need to pull all the pieces together. Like everyone, John and Sandy need to plan time to deal with these questions honestly. To develop a solid plan to carry them through their retirement years, they need to start where they are.

Achieve Your Dream—Action Step

What mindset do you live?

How do you know?

3

DISCOVER YOUR LIFE GOALS

Setting goals is the first step in turning the invisible into the visible.

—Tony Robbins

How do your life goals fit into your financial goals?

Early in my life, I developed some personal goals I review every morning. These goals, supported by my core values, determine everything I do and how I do them.

1. **Continue to develop my relationship with God and Jesus:** Learn all I can about Jesus by reading the Bible and praying. Strive to walk in His ways.
2. **Be a good husband to my wife, Julie:** Always treat her with the highest regard. Be empathetic to her daily duties and try to put myself in her place to understand what she's going through. Always maintain complete and open communication with her. Remember to think about her before I make any decisions in life. Show her daily how much I love her.
3. **Be a good father to my children:** Spend quality time with my children. Participate in as many events as

possible. Show them how much I love them daily. Teach them to be responsible citizens of this country and the world. Slow down my busy world to talk to and listen to these precious children. Always be there for them and let them know they can always depend on me.

4. **Maintain good physical and mental health:** Maintain a good diet. Do not eat or drink to dullness. Do not drink alcoholic beverages to excess. Exercise daily. To stay healthy mentally, I will always talk about my problems and emotions with someone I trust and seek advice for anything that troubles me.
5. **Become financially independent and self-reliant:** Work daily to improve my work and strive for excellence. Develop a good idea that will harbor financial independence.
6. **Be optimistic:** Always look at the glass as half full instead of half empty.
7. **Be honest:** Always tell the truth. Develop open relationships with everybody.
8. **Be frugal:** Spend only on needed items and when it does some good for somebody.
9. **Be competent:** Always strive to know the subject matter I am responsible for. Never claim to be all-knowing in areas I'm not properly prepared for or educated in.
10. **Grow intellectually:** Always strive to learn more about my subject matters of interest, and in those matters I need to know more about.
11. **Live by the Golden Rule (silence, sincerity, and justice):** Treat others the way I want to be treated. Speak not but what may benefit others or myself. Avoid trifling conversation. Do not wrong others through injury.
12. **Have confidence and integrity:** Live confidently, not in fear. Maintain strong integrity.

These twelve statements provide the guidelines as I plan my day, week, month, year—life. They help keep me on track and living the kind of life I desire.

We all benefit from spending time deciding how we want to live life. How can we know whether we have achieved our dreams without having first defined them? We cannot mark progress without having benchmarks and goals for which to strive.

This same goal-setting principle applies to your investment strategy. Being a family steward necessitates knowing your long-term plans as well as understanding present needs. To get where you want to go, you have to know where you are and where you're headed.

With that truth in mind, I conduct a personal interview with every new client. It's called a Discovery Meeting. The purpose is to uncover and understand my client's values, goals, key relationships, current advisors, desired level of involvement in financial planning, and personal interests. If my client is married, I ask both parties to answer the discovery questions. What we discover helps us identify decisions (good and bad) that have led to current circumstances as well as where my client wants to go next.

John and Sandy's meeting with the financial advisor seemed to be going well. Since this was a Discovery Meeting, they spent the time answering multiple questions and reviewing their current financial statements, investment portfolios, and debts. John and Sandy also discussed their dreams for their retirement years. John wanted to retire by 62 and Sandy a year or two later. They excitedly describe their new retirement home they hope to build on lakefront property.

When they talked about travel they'd like to do, Sandy shocked John with the number of places she wanted to visit.

While they both enjoyed travel, John looked forward to spending the majority of their time on the lake. He dreamed about fishing for hours, canoeing, and bonfires on the beach. What could be more beautiful?

Sandy, however, had a bucket list of places she'd dreamed about for years. Would their retirement planning allow them to provide for their family, care for their needs, and include travel? What was realistic?

Discover Your Dreams

As you begin your own goal-setting process or are reevaluating financial and legacy goals, I encourage you to take some time to conduct your own Discovery Meeting. If you are married, include your spouse.

It's easy to forget that our lives are the aggregate of every decision we have made. Our past decisions have helped create our present. As you consider the discovery questions, you might feel a tug of disappointment or perhaps a sense of failure. That's not the intent of this process. You can't change the past; remember that dwelling on regrets is a waste of time and energy.

You can change your future. But to do so, you must understand what led you to this point. This is where faith enters the picture. Do you believe you have hope for a bright future? I do, and my goal throughout this book and process is to help you grasp that faith and hope.

View this exercise as a fact-finding mission. You're gathering data to determine the best way to achieve your future goals. Without assessing your current status and desires, there is no plan or goal. Once you've made that assessment, answer this question, "What did I learn from my past decisions?" If you are married, this exercise helps you get on the same playing field. Discuss this with your spouse. Be open and authentic. Remember, this is your reality.

The good news? Your present reality doesn't dictate your future. This discovery process also helps you dream again, particularly if you've forgotten how. It allows you and your spouse to compare notes so you can work together to get to the same destination. One of the most important questions to consider in this process is *What's my (or our) next decision?*

Up until now, you may not have clear goals and objectives. That's okay. Today is a new day. My hope is that as you continue through this book, you'll discover hope for your future, understand the lessons you've learned from past decisions, and feel excitement about what lies ahead for you and your family.

Envision Your Future with Hope

So gather the facts and focus on the future. What are your hopes for your family—your legacy? Why are those dreams important to you? You have to know your *why* before you figure out the *how*.

Next, consider what actions are necessary to meet those stewardship goals. As Stephen Covey said, "Goals are pure fantasy unless you have a specific plan to achieve them." It's time for you to choose your target and define the road to get you there. When you meet with your financial advisor next, take your goals with you. Review them with your advisor and work together to develop a plan of action. My clients and I find this discovery information key to developing their Financial Goal Plan and Personal Financial Policy Statement, which we will discuss in the coming chapters.

ACHIEVE YOUR DREAM—ACTION STEP

Pause now and write out the answers to the discovery questions. I've included these questions in Appendix A as a fillable page. You can fill out an online version at MarkAhoFinancial.com/resources. If you're married, ask your spouse to fill them out as well. You may not be able to answer every question; that's okay. Just fill in as much information as possible.

Without understanding who you are and what you value, we can't develop a solid plan for your future. Therefore, as you start this process, write out the answers to these questions:

1. Values
   a. What's important to you about money?
   b. When you get to the end of your life, what values do you want to define your life?
2. Goals
   a. What are your personal goals for your life?
   b. What are your personal goals with your money?
3. Relationships
   a. What family relationships are most important to you?
   b. What is your religious orientation? How important are your relationships with people associated with your religion?
   c. Would you describe yourself as an introvert or an extrovert?
   d. What schools did you attend? How important is your relationship with these schools?
4. Advisors
   a. Do you have a lawyer? Do you want or need one?
   b. Who is your life insurance agent? If you don't have one, why not?

   c. Do you have a Tax Preparer (CPA) accountant?

5. Process
   a. How involved do you like to be in managing your finances?
   b. How often would you like to a review or have contact with your financial advisor? What's your preferred method of contact (phone, email, mail, text)?
6. Interests
   a. Do you follow sports? Which are your favorite teams?
   b. What are your favorite types of TV programs and movies?
   c. What do you read?
   d. Do you have health concerns or interests? What is your current health program?
   e. What are your hobbies?
   f. What would an ideal weekend or vacation be?
   g. What pets do you have?

PART 2

Original Game Plan

4
WHAT ISN'T WORKING?

The soul never thinks without a mental picture.

—Aristotle

What would happen in a basketball game if there were no coaches or referees? If you've played a pick-up game recently, you probably have a good idea. When the competition is high, it's tempting to throw out or disregard the rules to achieve our goal of winning.

Or maybe you're playing with others from a different country whose rules are slightly different. Was that recent interception the result of a foul or a shrewd play? You said the player fouled in his ball-handling because he clipped your arm. In their country, that move is legal. Who's right? Without pre-defined rules for the game, how do you know?

As for everything in life, there are rules to achieving our long-term goals. As a financial advisor, I'm wired to hoard your money to help you build wealth. Everything I do as a financial advisor comes from my deep faith in biblical abundance and in the future. My desire is to help you make the most of your money, so you have the ability to help people in need. I want to see your portfolio grow so you can equip your children with education so they can make a powerful impact on *their* children and grandchildren. To me, financial planning and building wealth isn't about building bigger storehouses but about being able to live and give generously.

Consider the following examples related to setting goals as we evaluate what's working in your financial life—and what isn't.

Unfocused Goals

After ten years of study and working long hours and barely making enough to survive, a new surgeon lands a real job. It might not be a dream job, but for the first time he or she is drawing a significant monthly salary. Finally, able to afford to buy a house and trade in the junker and get a better car, the surgeon now not only has school debts to repay but also the added expenses of a mortgage and car payment. Soon, the monthly expenses outpace the income. If the surgeon makes the regular monthly payments, the debt continues for thirty or forty years. There's no option to max out his 401(k), give generously to others, or build other investment opportunities.

You and your spouse work longs hours, but even though you scrimp and save as much as possible, there's more month than paycheck. Each month, you put just a small amount on your credit card to survive. You can't figure out another way to make ends meet. The increasing monthly debt results in greater stress.

As a careful family steward concerned about recent market losses, you've saved lots of money and put it in your bank's savings account. As you look back over the past five to ten years, the nominal interest rate hasn't kept up with the 2 percent inflation rate. When you factor in the income taxes you pay on the small interest income, inflation and taxes erode the pool of money.

Misinformation

A downturn in the market has the news media talking heads and some experts advising that you to sell your stocks and buy bonds. Media scare tactics sell, but you *want* to have faith in the future. You know that the market experiences a downturn every twelve to fifteen months, so you choose to think through your options logically, practice patience, and maintain discipline. You look at the real numbers over the time you initially wanted to invest your money and can see that if the market holds to its historic pattern, in time you will double or even triple your investments—if you don't pull your money out now. (This is what it means to be an investor. Instead of listening to the hype, you focus on your plan and objectives because being an investor is hard.)

The election put a new political party in office and the market gurus are up in arms. They incite panic with the message that the economy is sure to decline. You take a step back and weigh the myths against the facts. One myth hints that depending on which political party is in office, your investments will grow or decline. The fact is that history shows that whether Democrats, Republicans, or Independents are in office, the economy can grow under each ideology. That's the beauty of democracy. Winston Churchill[1] said, "Many forms of Government have been tried, and will be tried in this world of sin and woe. No one pretends that democracy is perfect or all-wise. Indeed it has been said that democracy is the worst form of Government except for all those other forms that have been tried from time to time. . . ." Though not perfect, because apart from God and Jesus nothing ever is, democracy allows for economic growth.

Overcoming False Beliefs Requires Focus

The scenarios in the preceding sections reveal the challenge of building wealth when we operate with unfocused goals or listen to myths rather than the facts. And I can understand how that happens. Life gets busy. When your only objective is to make it through each day, you make some decisions you don't realize have long-term financial strings attached. You're simply in the busy side of life with marriage, kids, work, and activities to juggle.

Life moves quickly, and when your focus is on maintaining the status quo, it's easy to focus on the wrong things. You prioritize things that aren't big rocks according to your values. Maybe challenges have thrown you off the path and bombarded you from every angle. Days, months, and even years can go by before you realize you've lost your focus. Financially, you've lost time and the advantage of compounding interest that could have happened during that time. You know that achieving your life plan will now require more money and sacrifice.

The good news is you *can* achieve your life plan. But you must choose to focus.

A saying I adopted years ago helps me focus each day: *I'm too busy to be sad, too positive to be doubtful, too optimistic to be fearful, and too determined to be defeated.*

During the discovery process, you will uncover what's important to you (goals) and how you think (objectives). Identifying your life plan sets the foundation for your future investments and wealth building. Zig Ziglar said, "If you aim at nothing, you will hit it every time." Sound financial planning by definition requires goals and objectives which is why a smart financial advisor takes significant time during the discovery process to help you identify what is most important to you.

As a financial advisor, my goal is to help clients envision the future differently. For many, this process allows them to, for the first time ever, imagine a bright future. I call this learning to see with the eyes of faith.

Once you've put in the time and effort to describe your preferred future, you will notice that your future looks different from your present. You see success instead of the same old thing. Your goal is attainable. And when you've made that mindset shift, my friend, you will know *now* is the time to get off the bench and into the game.

You'll also notice that with clear objectives, your game looks different. You've made a major adjustment in your game—a mindset shift. Magic happens when you bring your emotions and goals into alignment. You learn you don't adjust your investments based on current conditions no matter what media hype tells you.

You may discover, as some of my clients have, that it may not be possible to reach all of your financial goals and objectives. That's okay. All is not lost.

I spend time with my clients discussing how to reach what is attainable and figure out their Plan B. Our goal is to design an all-weather strategy (AWS) instead of trying to time the markets. I encourage you to do the same. An all-weather strategy allows you to stick to your plan and trust in the future, practice patience, and approach your goals with discipline.

> TIMING THE MARKET IS A FOOL'S GAME, WHEREAS TIME IN THE MARKET IS YOUR GREATEST NATURAL ADVANTAGE."—NICK MURRAY

Winning a championship basketball game requires setting objectives, drilling on the basics repeatedly, practicing the same movement for hours, trusting your teammates and coach to do their jobs, and working toward the same goal. By the time you get to that championship game, every movement is deeply ingrained in your muscles and thought patterns. You've prepared for the moment mentally, physically, and emotionally.

Just like a good coach, my goal as a financial planner is to move you from pessimism to optimism. You can reach your financial goals, wherever you may be in the game today. Read that sentence again: *You can reach your financial goals, wherever you may be in the game today.*

Do you believe it? I do. And I consider it a great privilege to guide you toward your desired future. Before you read on, take a few moments to thoughtfully answer the questions at the end of this chapter.

Achieve Your Dream—Action Step

Where have you abandoned your plans and objectives?

What caused you to become unfocused?

What is your next best step?

5

HOW TO BUILD YOUR FINANCIAL GOAL PLAN

Creativity is like looking at the world through a kaleidoscope. You look at a set of elements, the same ones everyone else sees, but then reassemble those floating bits and pieces into an enticing new possibility.

—Rosabeth Moss Kanter

After the Discovery Meeting, I build the client's Financial Goal Plan, which includes a Monte Carlo plan, a financial planning tool I use with all my clients. The Financial Goal Plan is simply a simulation that allows the financial advisor and investors to determine the size of the portfolio necessary to support their desired lifestyle. This plan takes into account inflation, life expectancy, rates of return, spending profile, tax rates, all sources of income like pensions and social security, and other specific factors.

To create a Financial Goal Plan, we take all the information the client provides during the Discovery Meeting and structure the plan following the client's stated retirement goals. If the first run of this Financial Goal Plan achieves the client's desired results, great. Often, however, we need to make adjustments. These changes help them meet their desired retirement goals.

Let's see what this looks like for John and Sandy.

⁂

The Greys made an appointment to meet with their financial advisor to review something called a Financial Goal Plan. This plan takes into account the six core principles for investing, along with their hopes and dreams for the future. It's a comprehensive plan based on statistics, numerous inputs, and careful analysis tailor-made for John and Sandy based on their future dreams, desires, and goals. Their financial advisor makes certain assumptions based on the Discovery Meeting.

Knowing that they want to retire in the next five to eight years, John and Sandy feel overwhelmed and quite unsure of their next steps. By this time in their life, they wanted to have certain financial goals completed:

- IRAs and 401(k) plans maxed out
- Home free and clear
- College savings account for each of their grandchildren
- Family trust

As stated earlier, they are considering selling their large family home. However, they need to make sure they are ready to move to the next phase of their life before making this commitment. They are considering building a new smaller home. Their dream is lakefront property, but neither are sure they have enough resources to make this dream a reality. They struggle with the questions, "Will my family and I be okay?" and "Can we live the life we want?"

A bit discouraged, John and Sandy review their accounts. By now, they expected larger balances. Where did they go wrong? The numbers don't seem to be enough. They're concerned the future won't look like their dreams.

The first thing their financial advisor reviews with them at their appointment following the Discovery Meeting are their value statements. The advisor reminds John and Sandy they do have faith in the future, which has made them good investors. Over the past thirty years, they've patiently weathered the many economic rollercoasters with a disciplined focus on their future. Because of this, their investments have done well. They didn't panic, withhold investing, or make rash decisions along the way. To answer their question, they've done well to this point.

Now they must consider whether their value statements still reflect their principles, desires, and goals. Reading the value statement thoroughly, John and Sandy realize it's still who they are and what they believe. There is no need to make any adjustment to this statement.

Diving into their newly developed Financial Goal Plan, their advisor reviews with them the assumptions he used. Everything in this document comes from the information they provided during the discovery process. Also factored into the assumptions in this plan are historical data for various investment options. While the data provides a good estimate, the results do not accurately predict or guarantee the future. Investing carries risks. These projected returns reflect the risk profile John and Sandy selected.

John and Sandy review the Net Worth Detail [see Figure 1] which is their current financial report card for their life to this point. It's simply a snapshot of the day their advisor created the goal plan. They've done well to diversify their funds into tax-deferred funds and after-tax accounts. The advisor points out their lack of debt remains a significant asset in their current financial blueprint.

Figure 1: Net Worth Summary

Net Worth Summary - All Resources

This is your Net Worth Summary as of 07/26/2021. Your Net Worth is the difference between what you own (your Assets) and what you owe (your Liabilities). To get an accurate Net Worth statement, make certain all of your Assets and Liabilities are entered.

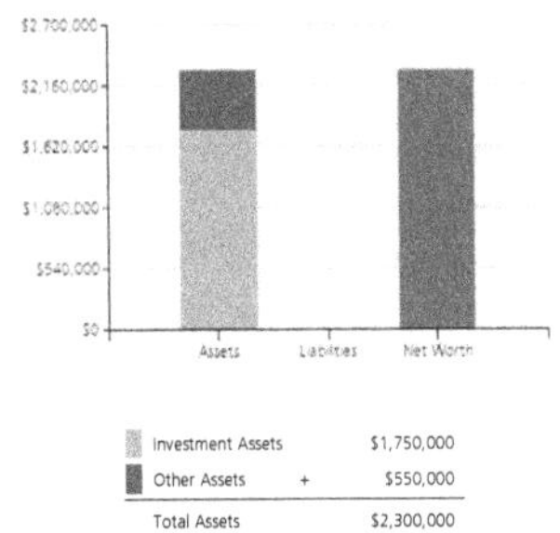

Investment Assets		$1,750,000
Other Assets	+	$550,000
Total Assets		$2,300,000
Total Liabilities	-	$0
Net Worth		$2,300,000

Description	Total
Investment Assets	
Employer Retirement Plans	$1,375,000
Taxable and/or Tax-Free Accounts	$375,000
Total Investment Assets:	**$1,750,000**
Other Assets	
Home and Personal Assets	$400,000
Business and Property	$150,000
Total Other Assets:	**$550,000**
Net Worth:	**$2,300,000**

See Important Disclosure Information section in this Report for explanations of assumptions, limitations, methodologies, and a glossary.

Prepared for : John and Sandy Grey Company: Raymond James Prepared by: Mark Aho
07/26/2021 Page 8 of 40

This case study is for illustrative purposes only. Individual cases will vary. Any information is not a complete summary or statement of all available data necessary for making an investment decision and does not constitute a recommendation. Prior to making any investment decision, you should consult with your financial advisor about your individual situation.

Because they are eager to see how their Financial Goal Plan projected their future options, the financial advisor explains the different scenarios and options. First they reviewed their current scenario [see Figure 2]. If they continue on their current course, their likelihood of funding their future goals has a 34 percent success rate.

Figure 2: Current Scenario

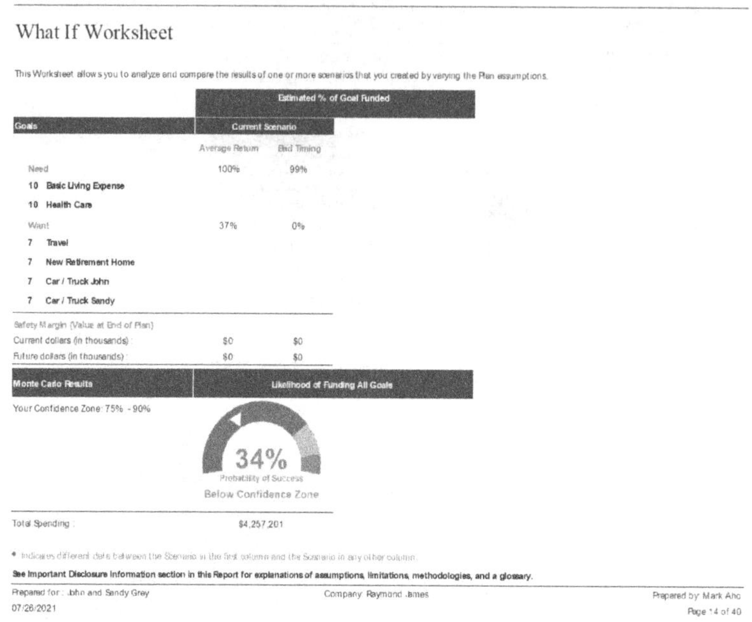

What If Worksheet

This Worksheet allows you to analyze and compare the results of one or more scenarios that you created by varying the Plan assumptions.

Goals	Estimated % of Goal Funded	
	Current Scenario	
	Average Return	Bad Timing
Need	100%	99%
10 Basic Living Expense		
10 Health Care		
Want	37%	0%
7 Travel		
7 New Retirement Home		
7 Car / Truck John		
7 Car / Truck Sandy		
Safety Margin (Value at End of Plan)		
Current dollars (in thousands) :	$0	$0
Future dollars (in thousands) :	$0	$0

Monte Carlo Results	Likelihood of Funding All Goals
Your Confidence Zone: 75% - 90%	34% Probability of Success Below Confidence Zone

Total Spending : $4,257,201

* Indicates different data between the Scenario in the first column and the Scenario in any other column.

See Important Disclosure Information section in this Report for explanations of assumptions, limitations, methodologies, and a glossary.

Prepared for : John and Sandy Grey | Company: Raymond James | Prepared by: Mark Aho
07/26/2021 | Page 14 of 40

This case study is for illustrative purposes only. Individual cases will vary. Any information is not a complete summary or statement of all available data necessary for making an investment decision and does not constitute a recommendation. Prior to making any investment decision, you should consult with your financial advisor about your individual situation.

That wasn't what they hoped to hear in this meeting. Worry set in quickly. It looks like they can't retire as planned, or they have to give up some of their retirement goals. Before they get too discouraged, their financial advisor reminds them their current scenario isn't fixed. They have several options to consider.

John and Sandy arrived at half-time. With their current numbers, it's time to review their goals and risk assessment to decide what changes, if any, they want to make to achieve their personal goals.

❧ ❧ ❧ ❧ ❧

Reviewing a Financial Goal Plan with your financial advisor provides opportunities you probably haven't considered at this point. Through my years of experience, I've found this tool extremely important for my family steward clients to answer the first two questions, "Will I be okay?" and "Can we live the life we want?" This tool also helps clients who've gotten off track or lost focus to see their possibilities to still achieve their goals and desires.

One university professor felt discouraged after a recent meeting with his financial advisor. He couldn't retire at sixty-two as he originally planned. But, after reviewing his Financial Goal Plan, and making some additional adjustments to other areas that impacted his financial outlook, he and his wife discovered they could still achieve their goals. It did mean a few more years of work, but much less than he feared. And, by taking advantage of other opportunities to acquire additional income streams, focusing their energies on the goal for a few more years, and delaying a few dream vacations, everything in their future desires became possible. They left this meeting relieved and excited.

I use the Financial Goal Plan which encapsulates the typical Monte Carlo Plan (see Appendix B). It is a risk assessment model that shows the probability of specific scenarios based on a client's stated desires. I love when family stewards view the different scenarios and realize they can achieve their desired financial results. So often, when it comes to our financial goals, we must make necessary adjustments. But the key to remember is the goal remains attainable in most cases.

Achieve Your Dream—Action Step

If you haven't met with your financial advisor in the past six months, schedule an appointment to review your financial dreams and goals. Request a Financial Goal Plan which includes a Monte Carlo plan. If you've lost focus, discuss what adjustments you can make now to help you achieve your future goals.

PART 3

Half-Time

6
WINNERS MAKE HALF-TIME ADJUSTMENTS

Never change a winning game; always change a losing one.

—Vince Lombardi

You cannot grow toward your goal if you don't assess where you are today. That's why we call this half-time.

What happens when a team goes into the locker room at half-time?

For at-home viewers, half-time appears to be longer than it is. Those watching the game might run to the restroom, grab a snack, mute the television, or even go for a quick walk. But for the players and coaches, half-time is used strategically.

If you are a player, you'll head to a certain location in the locker room depending on your position. There you'll meet with coaches to discuss strategy while trainers deal with immediate physical concerns. Due to time constraints, only the critical issues get addressed to the appropriate group of players. Someone on the team keeps a close eye on the time. In a matter of minutes, coaches articulate the necessary adjustments, and the players commit to the revised strategy.

When all players and coaches clearly understand what needs to happen to win the game, the team heads back to the field to play the second half—and win.

Half-time adjustments aren't major changes. Rather, they are minor tweaks to the established plan.

John and Sandy's financial advisor shows them options in a Financial Goal Plan [see Figure 3] which provide a much higher likelihood of success. (You can review this entire Financial Goal Plan in the pages of Appendix B.) The advisor shows them on their What If Worksheet that if they work until they are sixty-five and sixty-four, they increase their likelihood of funding all their goals from 34 percent to 84 percent. Adding three years of work brings significant changes to their projected future.

Figure 3: What If Worksheet

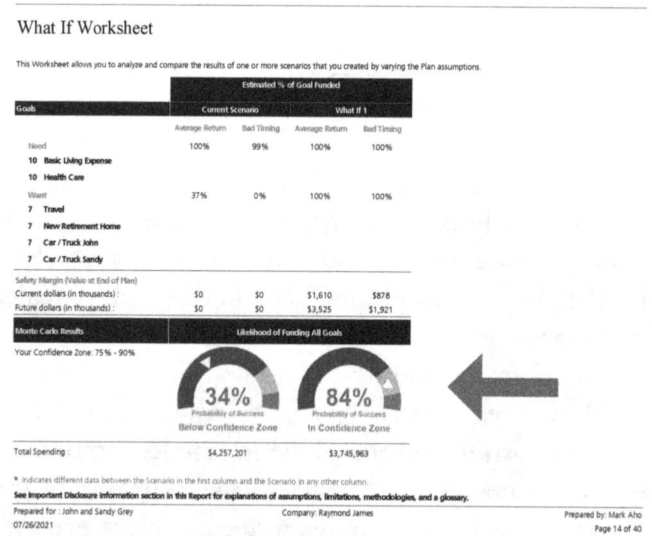

What If Worksheet

This Worksheet allows you to analyze and compare the results of one or more scenarios that you created by varying the Plan assumptions.

	Estimated % of Goal Funded			
Goals	Current Scenario		What If 1	
	Average Return	Bad Timing	Average Return	Bad Timing
Need	100%	99%	100%	100%
10 Basic Living Expense				
10 Health Care				
Want	37%	0%	100%	100%
7 Travel				
7 New Retirement Home				
7 Car / Truck John				
7 Car / Truck Sandy				
Safety Margin (Value at End of Plan)				
Current dollars (in thousands) :	$0	$0	$1,610	$878
Future dollars (in thousands) :	$0	$0	$3,525	$1,921

Monte Carlo Results	Likelihood of Funding All Goals	
Your Confidence Zone: 75% - 90%	34% Probability of Success Below Confidence Zone	84% Probability of Success In Confidence Zone
Total Spending :	$4,257,201	$3,745,963

* Indicates different data between the Scenario in the first column and the Scenario in any other column.

See Important Disclosure Information section in this Report for explanations of assumptions, limitations, methodologies, and a glossary.

Prepared for : John and Sandy Grey
07/26/2021

Company: Raymond James

Prepared by: Mark Aho
Page 14 of 40

This case study is for illustrative purposes only. Individual cases will vary. Any information is not a complete summary or statement of all available data necessary for making an investment decision and does not constitute a recommendation. Prior to making any investment decision, you should consult with your financial advisor about your individual situation.

Another option deals with adjustments to their investment portfolio. The financial advisor directs them to the line in their Model Portfolio Table [see Figure 4] marked AWS 70/30. This AWS 70/30 places 70 percent of their investments in diversified stocks and 30 percent in short to intermediate high-quality bonds. By increasing their stock investment portion of the portfolio by 20 percent and adjusting their cash and bond investments, their projected returns increase. But they also raise the volatility (risk) of their investments.

Their current portfolio has 50 percent in bonds and 50 percent in stocks. As family stewards, this conservative strategy felt more comfortable. To achieve their original goals, however, making small adjustments to their risk assessment yields more favorable results. Also, by working three more years, they continue adding to their 401(k) plans.

Another item their financial advisor suggested was a health savings account (HSA). The family contribution limit in 2021 is $7,200 per year. What is a health savings account? Simply stated, health savings accounts (HSAs) are like personal savings accounts, but the money in them is used to pay for health care expenses. You—not your employer or insurance company—own and control the money in your HSA. One benefit of an HSA is that the money you deposit into the account is not taxed.[1]

After some discussions with the Greys, they can maximize their contribution to their 401(k) plans, which is $26,000 per person, which does include their catch-up provision of $7,000. John and Sandy also realize they can come up with $5,100 to put into a health savings account (HSA).

Figure 4: Model Portfolio Table

Model Portfolio Table

The Risk-Based Portfolio was selected from this list of Portfolios, based upon the risk assessment. The Risk Band is comprised of the portfolio(s) that could be appropriate for you, based upon the Risk-Based Portfolio indicated. The Target Portfolio was selected by you. Refer to the Standard Deviation column in the chart below to compare the relative risk of your Current Portfolio to the Target Portfolio.

Portfolios	Name	Cash	Bond	Stock	Alternative	Unclassified	Projected Return	Standard Deviation
	Conservative	2.00%	68.00%	30.00%	0.00%	0.00%	3.94%	7.01%
■	Current	12.14%	37.86%	50.00%	0.00%	0.00%	4.25%	9.24%
	Conservative Balanced	2.00%	48.00%	50.00%	0.00%	0.00%	4.76%	9.92%
	(c) AWS 60/40 2	1.00%	39.00%	60.00%	0.00%	0.00%	5.20%	11.69%
▼	Balanced	2.00%	31.00%	67.00%	0.00%	0.00%	5.45%	12.79%
▲	(c) AWS 70/30 3	1.00%	29.00%	70.00%	0.00%	0.00%	5.61%	13.46%
	Balanced w/ Growth	2.00%	15.00%	83.00%	0.00%	0.00%	6.08%	15.46%
	Growth	2.00%	0.00%	98.00%	0.00%	0.00%	6.62%	17.93%

Risk Band ■ Current ▼ Risk-Based ▲ Target

Return vs. Risk Graph

When deciding how to invest your money, you must determine the amount of risk you are willing to assume to pursue a desired return. The Return versus Risk Graph reflects a set of portfolios that assume a low relative level of risk for each level of return, or conversely an optimal return for the degree of investment risk taken. The graph also shows the position of the Risk Band, Target, Risk-Based, and Custom Portfolios. The positioning of these portfolios illustrates how their respective risks and returns compare to each other as well as the optimized level of risk and return represented by the Portfolios.

This graph shows the relationship of return and risk for each Portfolio in the chart above.

Return

Risk (Standard Deviation)

Current Portfolio
Target (AWS 70/30 3)
Risk-Based Portfolio (Balanced)
Model Portfolios
Custom Portfolio(s)
Risk Band

See Important Disclosure Information section in this Report for explanations of assumptions, limitations, methodologies, and a glossary.

Prepared for : John and Sandy Grey
07/26/2021

Company: Raymond James

Prepared by: Mark Aho
Page 13 of 40

The investment profile is hypothetical, and the asset allocations are presented only as examples and are not intended as investment advice. Please consult with your financial advisor if you have questions about these examples and how they relate to your own financial situation.

Their financial advisor explains the goal isn't to build a financial plan that allows them to be okay. Rather, the desired outcome of their investment strategy is to live life with richness, give generously to their favorite charities and family, and achieve their legacy goals. He assures them if they will consider some of his suggestions, maintain their investor mindset, and decide on a plan and stick to it, their dreams for their retirement years and beyond are possible.

As they continued to review the Monte Carlo details, the Greys discover, with a few tweaks in their plans, their portfolio value would provide for their stated goals, allow them to travel, and continue to grow wealth over the next twenty-five to thirty years.

John and Sandy took the information home to discuss their options. Obviously, their current strategy needs some tweaks. Up until now, their investment portfolios had performed ahead of inflation. They looked at their original financial life goals as well. As they project a thirty-year plus retirement, John and Sandy decide that their original goal of retiring when John is sixty-two isn't realistic. To achieve other lifestyle and financial goals, they decide to work an additional three to five years to continue building their portfolio. They also started brainstorming other ideas to reduce their current expenses so they could increase their investments over the next ten years.

They pulled out the worksheets from their financial advisor, with all their notes, to work through their decision. Being people of faith, they prayed over this decision. Then, they looked at the four questions.

1. Will my family and I be okay? Yes, with these few tweaks.
2. Will my family and I be able to live the life we want? Yes, with these few tweaks.
3. Can I be generous to others? Yes.
4. Have I done enough? Yes, with these few tweaks.

Answering "yes" to each question can happen with a few tweaks. Adding three more years of work achieves all their goals. Relieved, John and Sandy realize they have done well and will use the next few years to further dial in their resources. Stopping to call their financial advisor to schedule their next appointment, they celebrate the foreseeable future.

John and Sandy also decide to interview builders and get their retirement home plans designed. They can use this time to finish the house, get moved in, and settled. Sandy loves this idea because they can spread out the big life changes over time so it won't feel as overwhelming. She loves her job and knows she'll experience some grief when she does retire.

Find an Advisor You Trust

By working with a qualified financial advisor who understands your long-term and lifestyle goals, a half-time assessment helps you identify where you need to make your tweaks. We've already discussed the discovery process, but half-time adjustments rely on the same principles.

A good financial advisor develops openness, freedom, and trust with you. They should have an iron-clad process for helping you build your investment portfolio. If you are to trust the insights your financial advisor brings to the table, you need a proven track record. Financial advisors charge a fee for their services, just like your doctor, dentist, or optometrist. Once you understand how paying a percentage to manage your financial assets, or more correctly, your financial behavior, could save you, you'll discover they are worth what they charge. While there are online robo-services that offer to manage your funds for a lower fee, they look strictly at asset allocation of your investments. A robo-advisor doesn't look at behavioral aspects to determine the best strategy to meet your individual needs. It's up to you which type of financial advisor you prefer.

Looking at where you are today, how does it line up with your personal value system and your existing financial policy statement? If you haven't written these, now is a good time to stop and complete these questionnaires in the Appendix or at MarkAhoFinancial.com. Don't worry if you've gotten a bit off track. Life does that to us. The beauty of this process is that you can make small adjustments at any time to achieve your desired goals.

WHAT IF YOU HAVEN'T DONE ENOUGH UP TO THIS POINT?

There are times when, for whatever reason, the goals you set early in life may not be possible as you first imagined them. Economic downturns happen which can result in a temporary drop in your portfolio. Depending on the strategy you've put in place, you might need to make a slight adjustment. Just as in our game illustration, usually these changes aren't major. Your financial advisor can help you with more accurate assessments and projections.

There are times, though, when your initial expectations can't be met. If that is the case, the question then becomes what needs to adjust—the expectations or the investment strategy?

If you feel like you can't win this game, it's time to make an appointment with your financial advisor to talk about a new strategy. It could be as simple as working a few years longer to build your portfolio. In most cases, there are ways to achieve your personal financial goals and principles. A qualified financial advisor helps you identify and implement these tweaks to your strategy.

Perhaps you've been playing the game without assistance. Good for you for diving in and working hard to create a solid financial portfolio. But if you find yourself in this half-time period discouraged and concerned about your future, now may be the perfect time to connect with a qualified financial advisor who understands your goals.

When you're in these half-time adjustments, it's important to remember the six guiding principles:

- Have faith in the future.
- Be patient.
- Be disciplined.
- Determine Asset Allocation.

- Focus on Diversification.
- Practice Annual Rebalancing.

A financial advisor's goal is to help you build and preserve wealth so you can live abundantly and generously. Don't get discouraged if you aren't as far along as you thought you would be or if market fluctuations are wreaking havoc on your portfolio. Even during economic downturns, you can build wealth. As a family steward, you have hopes and dreams for your family and future. And, because of your convictions, you work with your advisor to make adjustments today that will build wealth for the future so you can meet not only your needs but also your family's. With the advice of a trustworthy advisor, you can remain hopeful because you know the work you've put into your long-term plans.

According to Nick Murray in his book, *Simple Wealth, Inevitable Wealth*, "Optimism, is, in fact, the only long-term realism." When clients ask if they can meet their lifestyle and financial goals, I point them back to their outlook. Do they believe there is hope for their future? That's key to anyone's success. Without faith in the future, where would any of us be?

The coach's job is to get you back on the field. As a financial advisor, my job is to help you accurately assess today and design the next steps to create the future you desire. Now it's your turn to take the next step.

Achieve Your Dream—Action Step

What half-time adjustments do you need to make? Write them down. Be specific.

7

WHAT MAKES A STRONG INVESTMENT PORTFOLIO?

Permanence, perseverance and persistence in spite of all obstacles, discouragements, and impossibilities: It is this, that in all things distinguishes the strong soul from the weak.

—Thomas Carlyle

Investors have faith in the future. They develop a strategy, a Financial Goal Plan, and stick to it. A true investor doesn't emotionally react to market fluctuations. They understand the historical nature of investing. With the help of their financial advisor, they've built a solid plan and trust that plan.

To state it simply, investors choose investments that create wealth steadily over the long haul. Those investments include time-tested stocks, bonds, cash, and real estate. I include this Ibbotson chart [see Figure 5] to illustrate how these types of investments perform over a seventy-five year period.

Figure 5: Ibbotson Chart

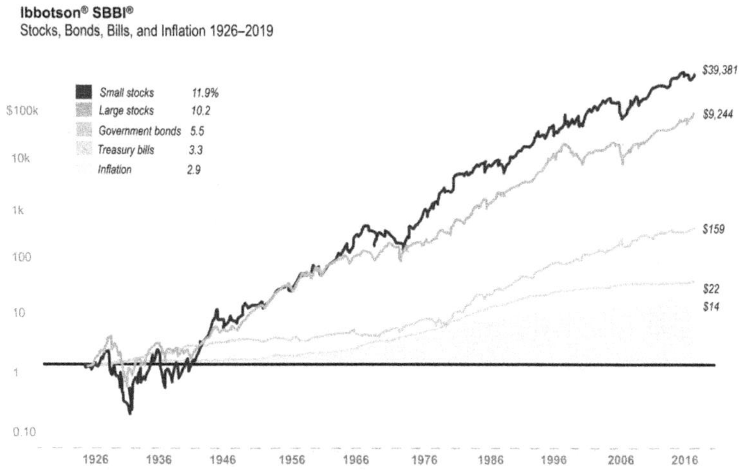

This is a hypothetical example for illustration purpose only and does not represent an actual investment.

As you can see in the Ibbotson chart [see Figure 5], there is a stark difference in the returns of equities versus bonds and cash. When you consider longer periods, this difference creates a great impact on your total wealth. What the investor gives up with bonds and cash is stability—low or no volatility—with his hard-earned dollars. What he gains by investing in stocks is the possibility of a much larger investment portfolio. To illustrate this more fully, let's look at a core equity portfolio versus a bond portfolio.

Two Investment Strategies

There's no such thing as the perfect investment, but we can put together strategies that seem more preferable than others. The two strategies to review are the twenty-year bond and the growing dividend stock portfolio.

First, the twenty-year bond strategy [see Figure 6]. To keep it simple, we'll use an investment of $100,000 that pays a generous yield of 5 percent. Basic math means you earn $5,000 per year on this investment, which you can use for living expenses. At the end of the twenty-year period, you still have your initial $100,000. However, when you factor in inflation (we'll use 2.2 percent for this illustration), your initial $100,000 investment value has decreased to $64,711.59. While your money remained safe and you earned interest over the twenty years, the actual buying power of those funds decreased due to inflation.

Figure 6: Twenty-Year Bond Strategy

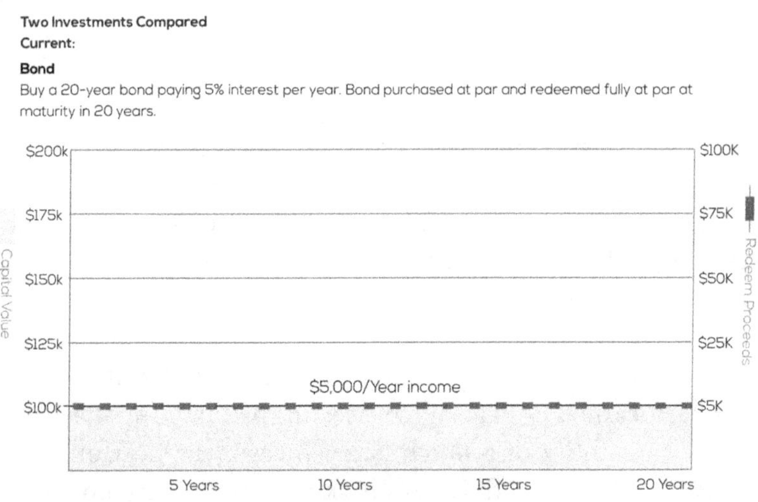

Second, the growing dividend stock portfolio strategy (GDSP) [see Figure 7]. We'll use the same $100,000 initial investment. In this plan, we invest the money in twenty-five high-quality companies who have paid and grown their dividends every year for several years. For our illustrative purposes, we estimate the total dividend payout is around 3 percent. In year one, your dividend payout is $3,000. That's

$2,000 less that year than with the bond strategy. Remember, however, the purpose of this GDSP plan is growth.

If the average rate of dividends paid increases by 6 percent per year for all twenty years, then in year twenty, the amount of dividends paid is $9,621.41. Let's also say the capital appreciation of the stocks is 6 percent per year. Therefore, 3 percent is paid out for living expenses, and the growth of capital remains in the account. This would indicate the pot of money would have grown to $320,714.

Figure 7: Growing Divident Stock Portfolio (GDSP)

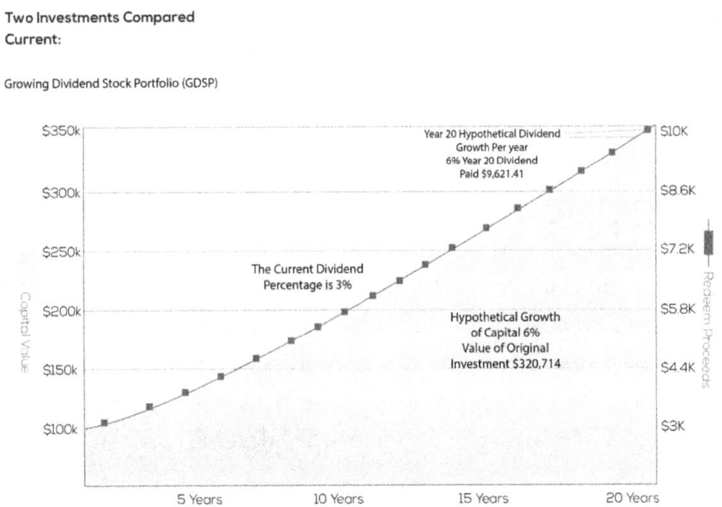

This investment does not have a stated maturity date. The income therefore can continue and has grown to 9.6% of the original investment.

Compliance Note: This is a hypothetical situation and is not intended to reflect the actual performance of any particular security. Future performance cannot be guaranteed, and investment yields will fluctuate with market conditions. Actual investor results will vary.

Compliance Note: Dividends are not guaranteed and must be authorized by the company's board of directors.

While this increase might sound too good to be true, the illustrative numbers are conservative. Using the return of the S&P Dividend Aristocrats[1] actual performance from January 31, 1990 to December 31, 2018, the rate was 11.6 percent. Even with my conservative estimate, the GDSP strategy still blows away the bond strategy.

Which strategy would you rather own? Choice A is the bond, where you get your money back and $5,000 per year over twenty years. Choice B is the growing dividend stock portfolio, where you get a steadily increasing amount of income over twenty years, in which the amount is almost double of Choice A by the end of the term. Plus, you get a capital base that has almost tripled.

Let's review some basic building blocks. For a more comprehensive explanation, read *Generations of Wealth* or make an appointment with your financial advisor to review your options.

Mutual Funds

Mutual funds can be stocks, bonds, or cash. It is a professionally managed investment program that provides diversification for small investors. They can be a good mixture of all the building blocks for the average investor who otherwise wouldn't have the necessary resources to get proper diversification.

Exchange-Traded Funds (ETFs)

Exchange-traded funds are gaining in popularity. To provide you with a textbook definition from *Investopedia*[2], an ETF is "a marketable security that tracks an index, a commodity, bonds, or a basket of assets like an index fund. Unlike mutual funds, an ETF trades like a common stock on a stock exchange. ETFs experience price changes throughout the day as they are bought and sold."

Compliance Note: Investors should carefully consider the investment objectives, risks, charges and expenses of mutual funds and exchange-traded funds before investing. The prospectus and summary prospectus contains this and other information about these registered investment company products. The prospectus and summary prospectus is available from your financial advisor and should be read carefully before investing.

Individual Stocks

Companies of all types are listed on various stock exchanges such as the New York Stock Exchange. If you want to invest in a certain company, do so. I know people who invested in startup companies because they believed in their product or mission. It is satisfying to take a chance on a company, watch it grow, and reap some financial rewards as well.

Stocks break down into *value* or *growth* stocks.

1. ***Value stocks*** trade at a lower price than their dividends, sales, and earnings would indicate. You hear these stocks referred to as large capitalization (market value greater than $10 billion), small capitalization (market value of $300 million to $2 billion), mid-capitalization (market value between $2 billion to $10 billion), and micro-small capitalization (market under $300 million).
2. ***Growth stocks*** generally deal with new ideas, technology, and products. They are momentum-oriented with a fast-expected growth rate of earnings. Often these can be riskier than value stocks, but the potential can be far greater and worth the risk.

Smart investors build diversification through blending investments in value and growth stock classification, which helps balance your portfolio.

Bonds

Bonds result when a company, government, or municipality needs to raise money for a specific purpose. Types of bonds include short, intermediate, and long duration; government, corporate, and mortgage-backed; global country, global corporate, and globally blended. When you invest in bonds, you finance those projects which makes you a creditor.

A well-balanced portfolio includes a percentage of bonds. They provide a lower risk component. This portion of the portfolio allows you to draw funds as necessary, especially during retirement.

Cash

The last basic building block to discuss is cash, which can be in the form of a money market or certificate of deposit (CD). There's little return but minimal principal volatility with cash savings. CDs of less than one year would be considered cash and offer similarly low returns with virtually no principal loss risk. Any CD that is over a year would be considered a bond.

A good financial advisor will help you rebalance your portfolio annually to keep it within the stated guidelines of the financial goal plan.

Looking at John and Sandy Grey's current portfolio allocation [see Figure 8], you see how their investments break down. They currently have 50 percent in stocks and 50 percent in cash and bonds.

Figure 8: Current Portfolio Allocation - John & Sandy Grey

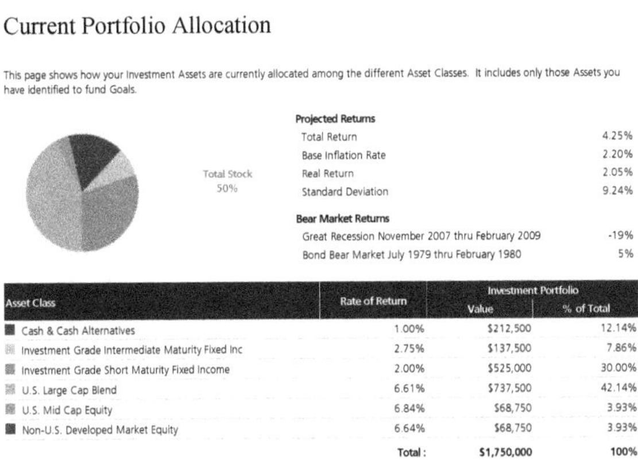

Current Portfolio Allocation

This page shows how your Investment Assets are currently allocated among the different Asset Classes. It includes only those Assets you have identified to fund Goals.

Projected Returns

Total Return	4.25%
Base Inflation Rate	2.20%
Real Return	2.05%
Standard Deviation	9.24%

Bear Market Returns

Great Recession November 2007 thru February 2009	-19%
Bond Bear Market July 1979 thru February 1980	5%

Asset Class	Rate of Return	Investment Portfolio Value	% of Total
Cash & Cash Alternatives	1.00%	$212,500	12.14%
Investment Grade Intermediate Maturity Fixed Inc	2.75%	$137,500	7.86%
Investment Grade Short Maturity Fixed Income	2.00%	$525,000	30.00%
U.S. Large Cap Blend	6.61%	$737,500	42.14%
U.S. Mid Cap Equity	6.84%	$68,750	3.93%
Non-U.S. Developed Market Equity	6.64%	$68,750	3.93%
	Total :	**$1,750,000**	**100%**

See Important Disclosure Information section in this Report for explanations of assumptions, limitations, methodologies, and a glossary.

Prepared for : John and Sandy Grey
07/26/2021

Company: Raymond James

Prepared by: Mark Aho
Page 9 of 40

This case study is for illustrative purposes only. Individual cases will vary. Any information is not a complete summary or statement of all available data necessary for making an investment decision and does not constitute a recommendation. Prior to making any investment decision, you should consult with your financial advisor about your individual situation.

As part of their half-time adjustment, their financial advisor reviews this current plan and makes recommendations. Their current allocations will not help them achieve their desired goals. One of those recommendations means moving from 50 percent bonds and 50 percent stocks to 30 percent bonds and 70 percent stocks. This re-allocation of the financial goal plan means accepting more volatility along with receiving greater potential rewards.

ACHIEVE YOUR DREAM—ACTION STEP

Review your current investment portfolio. How well diversified are you? Schedule a meeting with your financial advisor to review a recent Financial Goal Plan.

8
HOW DO SOCIAL SECURITY AND MEDICARE BENEFITS AFFECT THE HALF-TIME ADJUSTMENTS?

Work as if you were to live a hundred years.
Pray as if you were to die tomorrow.

—Benjamin Franklin

With these new facts to review, John and Sandy's financial advisor also brought up the topic of Social Security and Medicare benefits. Having not considered this before, the Greys realized they needed more information and then time to discuss the impact. Their financial advisor began by explaining the following options[1]:

- Start at age 62, receive 75 percent of your total benefit amount per month
- Start at age 66 and 10 months, receive 100 percent of your total benefit amount per month

- Start at age 70, receive 125 percent of your total benefit amount per month

What does this mean? Let's say John's monthly retirement benefit is $1000, to keep the math in simple round numbers. If he elects to take his benefit at age 62, his monthly benefit is approximately $750. At age 66 and 10 months, John receives the full $1000 per month in benefit. But, if he elects to wait until age 70, John's monthly benefit amount is approximately $1,250.

John and Sandy discussed these Social Security options with their financial advisor. Could they wait to use these benefits until age seventy if they retired at sixty-five and sixty-four respectively? What retirement goals and dreams became more probable if they worked longer than sixty-five and sixty-four? As they processed this information, new options became clear and their excitement rose.

When Should You Take Social Security?

Knowing when to take Social Security benefits to best support your long-term goals takes some study and discussion with your financial advisor. I include the following information to help you navigate this decision with information that is current as of the writing of this book. For the most current information, please visit ssa.gov and other reliable sources. Your financial advisor can help you as well.

Social Security retirement benefits payments can begin as early as age sixty-two. You can apply once you reach sixty-one years and nine months of age.

Should you opt to take Social Security at the earliest option, the Social Security Administration (SSA)[1] reduces your payments if you start collecting before your full retirement age, or FRA. (FRA is currently sixty-six and two months. The current plan involves gradually increasing the age to sixty-seven for people born in 1960 or later.) Once you reach your FRA, you qualify for 100 percent of your basic monthly benefit, which the SSA calculates based on your thirty-five highest-earning years.

However, to gain the maximum payment and accrue delayed retirement credits, wait until age seventy to apply. (You can apply later than seventy, but it doesn't change your benefit.) Discuss these options with your financial advisor who will help you take into account your entire retirement portfolio as part of the decision process.

Here are other factors to help determine the best starting age to receive benefits:

Spousal Benefits: Is your spouse currently receiving retirement benefits? Then your claim based on their work record can begin at sixty-two.

Survivor Benefits: You can apply for these benefits on the record of a deceased spouse or ex-spouse at sixty. If you are disabled, you can claim these benefits at fifty. Or, you can claim the benefits at any age if you are caring for your deceased spouse's under-sixteen or disabled child.

Social Security Disability Insurance

With no minimum age requirement to receive Social Security Disability Insurance, you may qualify for these benefits without meeting the workforce time requirements. Your application for these benefits must demonstrate that your medical condition meets the SSA's strict definition of disability and that you cannot work due to the disability. According to the inspector general's 2018 report[2], the SSA faces a huge backlog of pending disability cases. If you wonder if you might qualify for these benefits, please visit ssa.gov and select the disability section to understand the requirements and process.

Perhaps the more valuable question to consider is when you should claim benefits rather than when you can receive benefits. When to claim them is a complicated answer that depends on your job situation, family circumstances, financial planning, physical health, and other factors. Again, review all your options with your financial advisor to make the best decision for your situation.[3]

How Long Do You Have to Work to Get Social Security?

You need forty Social Security credits to qualify for retirement benefits. Each year of employment you can earn up to four by paying Social Security tax on your income.

Look at this earning example to help understand how you earn credits. In 2021, $1,470 in earnings equals one credit. After you make $5,880 for the year, you earn four credits. When looking at your eligibility, it doesn't matter how long it takes you to earn your forty credits. Typically, after a decade of being in the workforce, most people qualify for Social Security benefits.

What about qualifying for Social Security Disability Insurance (SSDI)? If you are unable to work due to a significant health issue, please go to ssa.gov and select the Disability section. SSDI can require as few as six credits for a person under twenty years old. But if you are sixty-two or over, the requirements may be much higher. The number of credits required depends on the age you became disabled. I suggest you access the Social Security publication "How You Can Earn Credits"[4] for complete information.

The Supplemental Security Income (SSI) provides another assistance program to adults and children with disability or blindness who meet certain criteria. This program, funded by general tax revenues rather than Social Security taxes, provides monthly income to help meet basic needs like food, clothing, and shelter. Since the requirements for this program change regularly, and vary from individual to individual, please visit ssa.gov/benefits/ssi for complete information.

Finally, understand that the minimum income required to earn work credits also changes annually based on national wage trends. Your best option is to visit ssa.gov to get the most current information. If you have not earned sufficient credits to qualify for Social Security benefits on your own, you may receive some benefits based on your spouse's record or a parent's record. Again, visit ssa.gov for the requirements.

Getting Started with Medicare

Your best source for information about Medicare is medicare. gov. Medicare is the federal health insurance program for:

- People who are sixty-five or older
- Certain younger people with disabilities
- People with End-Stage Renal Disease (permanent kidney failure requiring dialysis or a transplant, sometimes called ESRD) or ALS (also known as Lou Gehrig's disease)

As with the Social Security information, I include the following to help you understand the basics about your Medicare benefits under the rules as of this writing. Please visit Medicare.gov for the most current information. Review this with your financial advisor.

5 Important Facts about Medicare[5]

1. Some people get Medicare automatically, and some have to sign up. You may have to sign up if you're sixty-five (or almost sixty-five) and not getting Social Security.
2. There are certain times of the year when you can sign up or change how you get your coverage.
3. If you sign up for Medicare Part B when you're first eligible, you can avoid a penalty.
4. You can choose how you get your Medicare coverage.
5. You may be able to get help with your Medicare costs.

Before you get into the details, it's important to understand some basic information about Medicare and how it can help you cover the costs of your health care. It might be different than you think! Here's a brief explanation of how Medicare works, what it covers, and a comparison of the two main ways to get your Medicare coverage. The different parts of Medicare help cover specific services:

- **Medicare Part A (Hospital Insurance)**

  Part A covers inpatient hospital stays, care in a skilled nursing facility, hospice care, and some home health care.
- **Medicare Part B (Medical Insurance)**

  Part B covers certain doctors' services, outpatient care, medical supplies, and preventive services.
- **Medicare Part D (prescription drug coverage)**

  Part D helps cover the cost of prescription drugs (including many recommended shots or vaccines).

How Does Medicare Work?

With Medicare, you have options in how you get your coverage. Once you enroll, you'll need to decide how you'll get your Medicare coverage. There are two main ways:

1. Original Medicare

   Original Medicare includes Medicare Part A (Hospital Insurance) and Medicare Part B (Medical Insurance). You pay for services as you get them. When you get services, you'll pay a deductible at the start of each year, and you usually pay 20 percent of the cost of the Medicare-approved service, called coinsurance. If you want drug coverage, you can add a separate drug plan (Part D).

   Original Medicare pays for much, but not all, of the cost for covered health care services and supplies. A Medicare Supplement Insurance (Medigap) policy can help pay some of the remaining health care costs, like copayments, coinsurance, and deductibles. Some Medigap policies also cover services that Original Medicare doesn't cover, like medical care when you travel outside the U.S.

2. Medicare Advantage

   Medicare Advantage is an "all in one" alternative to Original Medicare. These "bundled" plans include Part A, Part B, and usually Part D. Most plans offer extra benefits that Original Medicare doesn't cover, such as vision, hearing, dental, and more. Medicare Advantage Plans have yearly contracts with Medicare and must follow Medicare's coverage rules. The plan must notify you about any changes before the start of the next enrollment year.

Each Medicare Advantage Plan can charge different out-of-pocket costs. They can also have different rules for how you get services.

Medicare Prescription Drug Coverage (Part D)

Medicare drug coverage helps pay for prescription drugs you need. To get Medicare drug coverage, you must join a Medicare-approved plan that offers drug coverage (this includes Medicare drug plans and Medicare Advantage Plans with drug coverage).

Each plan can vary in cost and specific drugs covered, but must give at least a standard level of coverage set by Medicare. Medicare drug coverage includes generic and brand-name drugs. Plans can vary the list of prescription drugs they cover (called a formulary) and how they place drugs into different "tiers" on their formularies.

Plans have different monthly premiums. You'll also have other costs throughout the year in a Medicare drug plan. How much you pay for each drug depends on which plan you choose.

* * * * *

The Greys reviewed their Social Security options with their financial advisor. After weighing all their options, they decide to take Social Security at their full retirement age. It makes sense with their overall goal plan.

And, with their stated desire to travel as long as possible, they opt to take the original Medicare plan and purchase a Medigap policy as well.

ACHIEVE YOUR DREAM—ACTION STEP

How does Social Security and Medicare fit into your overall Financial Goal Plan? Review the websites listed in this chapter. Jot some notes here, along with questions you need to review with your financial advisor.

PART 4

New Game Plan

9

DESIGNING YOUR PERSONAL FINANCIAL POLICY STATEMENT

Our goals can only be reached through a vehicle of a plan, in which we must fervently believe, and upon which we must vigorously act. There is no other route to success.

—Pablo Picasso

Having made their decision to adjust their retirement age and follow their financial advisor's investment portfolio adjustments, John and Sandy scheduled their appointment to review the new Personal Financial Policy Statement.

So, what exactly is a Personal Financial Policy Statement (PFPS)? It is the document that puts the client and the financial advisor on the same page. It provides a full understanding of the client's financial and life goals and objectives. This document is created from the information in the Discovery Meeting and completed after the client approves the goal plan (Financial Goal Plan) with the adjustments made to reach acceptable goals. This bedrock document defines the path the client and the financial advisor will follow for the foreseeable future. Any changes are only made with the full approval of the client. Changes do occur from time to time since the world changes and, of course, changes in the client's life may necessitate some adjustments.

The core of the Greys' financial retirement plan is their years of saving and investing in both taxable and tax-free accounts otherwise known as brokerage accounts, which are after-tax funds and their tax-deferred investments such as 401(k) plans and IRAs as seen on their Net Worth Detail [see Figure 9].

Figure 9: Net Worth Detail

Net Worth Detail - All Resources

This is your Net Worth Detail as of 07/26/2021. Your Net Worth is the difference between what you own (your Assets) and what you owe (your Liabilities). To get an accurate Net Worth statement, make certain all of your Assets and Liabilities are entered.

Description	John	Sandy	Joint	Total
Investment Assets				
Employer Retirement Plans				
401(k)	$850,000			$850,000
401(k)		$525,000		$525,000
Taxable and/or Tax-Free Accounts				
Taxable Investment Account			$375,000	$375,000
Total Investment Assets:	**$850,000**	**$525,000**	**$375,000**	**$1,750,000**
Other Assets				
Home and Personal Assets				
Home			$325,000	$325,000
Personal Property			$75,000	$75,000
Business and Property				
New home property			$70,000	$70,000
Texas Condo	$80,000			$80,000
Total Other Assets:	**$80,000**	**$0**	**$470,000**	**$550,000**
Net Worth:				**$2,300,000**

See Important Disclosure Information section in this Report for explanations of assumptions, limitations, methodologies, and a glossary.

Prepared for : John and Sandy Grey
07/26/2021

Company: Raymond James

Prepared by: Mark Aho
Page 7 of 40

This case study is for illustrative purposes only. Individual cases will vary. Any information is not a complete summary or statement of all available data necessary for making an investment decision and does not constitute a recommendation. Prior to making any investment decision, you should consult with your financial advisor about your individual situation.

At this point of the review, John and Sandy have some questions about not only growing wealth but also preserving their assets. Being in their fifties, they feel differently about their investments and about risk landscapes. Their financial advisor takes this opportunity to explain two basic types of risk.

First, there is the risk of losing principal. This happens when markets have some negative volatility and, at least on a temporary basis, the overall value of their investment portfolio decreases in value.

The second risk, however, is the more important one to consider. This is the loss of future buying power or what is called "ongoing inflation." This entails considering the cost of what basic goods are today versus the future. If your investment portfolio does not grow at least at the rate of inflation you are most likely going backwards.

The financial advisor reminds the Greys that he is planning for thirty years or more of retirement for them. Therefore, reduction in purchasing power is the top risk he considers for their investment assets. He points out, too, that their emergency funds must be invested in short-term fixed income or cash to preserve the principal.

Their financial advisor welcomes the opportunity to review two investment strategies with them.

The first strategy is to invest their after-tax investments in a managed core individual stock portfolio with some satellite exchange-traded funds. This portfolio has relatively low turnover and includes high quality growing dividend companies. In this strategy, the core is surrounded by other types of assets, such as fixed income, small capitalization companies, and developed international and emerging markets. [See Figure 10. As of this writing, both dividends and capital gains are taxed at 15 percent for a married couple filing a joint return with total income of less than $501,600. This tax rate increases to 20 percent for income levels over $501,600 for joint income filers.]

Figure 10: Managed Core Individual Stock Strategy

The second strategy is designed for the tax-deferred/401(k) investments. It is a diversified portfolio of equities and bonds. The Greys' goal plan has been adjusted to have 70 percent in diversified equites and 30 percent in diversified bonds and cash. These investments are all in either actively managed mutual funds/exchange-traded funds or passive mutual funds/exchange-traded funds. We'll review the breakdown of strategic asset allocation in the investment portfolio asset allocation overview in the pages ahead.

The Greys use mutual funds in this strategy because these funds offer great diversification and management. There are no yearly tax issues since all earnings and capital gains are tax-deferred. When the Greys start to take distributions from these tax-deferred accounts in the future, all distributions taken will be distributed as ordinary income.

What Do You Do with Your 401(k) or 403(b) Post-Retirement?

According to irs.gov[1], a 401(k) plan is a qualified profit-sharing plan where an employee contributes a portion of their wages to individual accounts. These investments are excluded from your taxable income unless you opt for designated Roth deferrals. Many employers include as part of their employee compensation packages regular contributions to their employees' accounts. When withdrawals are taken, ideally after age 59 ½, you as the employee will pay taxes on the distributions from this account.

Similar to 401(k) plans, a 403(b) plan[2], also known as a tax-sheltered annuity (TSA), is a retirement plan offered by public schools and certain 501(c)(3) tax-exempt organizations. If you work for a non-profit, your employer plan is most likely a 403(b) plan. Like a 401(k) plan, your deferred salary goes into an individual account and is not subject to federal and state income tax until you take a distribution. Many 403(b) plans also include a Roth option. Funds contributed to a Roth portion of the plan are taxable currently but tax-free, including any earnings, when distributed.

A financial advisor looks through the cost structure of the specific employer plan as well as factors in your life goals and objectives to help you make wise decisions about how to manage your employer plans in retirement. If you haven't already secured a financial advisor, make sure you find one several years before retirement and have this discussion with them. It is important to map out how to reach your goals and objectives for retirement to determine what the right path is for your employer plan.

Most financial planners will advise you to move your 401(k) or 403(b) money at your retirement into an Individual Retirement Account (IRA) for a few reasons. First, they can't manage the money because it is in a program they can't access. Second, because they can't manage the money, they cannot be compensated with fees for advice regarding an established

401(k) or 403(b). This means that if you choose to leave your 401(k) or 403(b) funds in its existing plan, you will most likely have to manage your own portfolio.

If you choose to take your money out of the 401(k) or 403(b) plan, you can roll it over to a tax-deferred IRA. Your financial advisor invests the proceeds according to your Financial Goal Plan. Always review your available options, fees, and features of each before moving your retirement assets.

Compliance Note: In addition to rolling over your 401(k) or 403(b) to an IRA, there are other options. For additional information and what is suitable for your particular situation, please consult a qualified financial advisor.

Here is a brief look at the options for your 401(k) or 403(b):

1. Leave the money in your former employer's plan if permitted.
   - Pros: If you like the investments in the plan, you get to stay in them, and you may not incur a fee for leaving it in the plan. This choice does not constitute a taxable event.
2. If you aren't retiring, but leaving the company, you could roll over the assets to your new employer's plan, if one is available and it is permitted.
   - Pros: You can keep it all together and have a larger sum of money working for you. This also does not constitute a taxable event.
   - Con: Not all employer plans accept rollovers.
3. Rollover to an IRA.
   - Pros: You likely have more investment options. It allows for the consolidation of accounts and locations. This also does not constitute a taxable event.
   - Cons: There is usually a fee involved. There might be potential fees for termination.
4. Cash out the account.
   - Cons: Cashing out is a taxable event, and there is a potential for loss of investments. This is a costly option for individuals

under fifty-nine-and-one-half years of age. You'll pay a ten percent penalty in addition to being subject to applicable income taxes.

If you elect to roll the money out of your 401(k) or 403(b) plan and into an investment option under the management of an advisory firm, then the financial advisor can go over your strategy throughout retirement. They will map out a plan for you into your nineties. With advances in healthcare, they may need to move your healthcare numbers higher. Nonetheless, I know plenty of people who are over ninety years old, so running numbers to that age makes plenty of sense.

WHAT ABOUT ROTH IRAS?

As part of the discussion with your financial advisor about your employer plan funds, you have the option to move part or all of the 401(k) or 403(b) funds into an IRA. Per irs.gov, an IRA is a tax-deferred investment to provide financial security for your retirement. Traditional Individual Retirement Accounts are personal savings plans where contributions may be tax deductible. When discussing your options with your financial advisor, another item you might consider is moving money from your IRA to a Roth IRA, which may be beneficial to maximize a current lower tax bracket.

Young people, especially those in a lower tax bracket, may benefit from contributing to a Roth 401(k) or Roth IRA. By taking advantage of this retirement investment option, a young person pays the taxes on monies when they invest them. Those funds grow tax-free, including all earnings. Upon their retirement, those distributions are tax-free. Retired people, however, may want to consider moving money from their IRA to a Roth IRA, especially if they are in a lower tax bracket. If you have the monies available to pay the taxes at the time you move the funds from a traditional IRA to a Roth IRA, you could save on future tax implications. Remember, Roth 401(k) or Roth IRAs distributions come out income-tax free. This can be beneficial in future years.

Discuss your options with your financial advisor prior to your retirement. Get your strategy in place to maximize your wealth building potential.

John and Sandy asked a few more clarifying questions. Their financial advisor answered each one, reminding them this is a lifetime strategy they review every year together and make adjustments to as necessary. They review the Personal Financial Policy Statement which their financial advisor built based upon their input, financial goals, and preferred adjustments to their allocations. Like a good coach, he walks them through the adjustments. Just because everything isn't perfect doesn't mean John and Sandy change their direction and focus. They lean into their faith in the future. The goal will be attained.

John and Sandy Grey's Personal Financial Policy Statement (PFPS)

This is a sample PFPS for illustrative purposes only.

Advisory Support Team

- Financial Advisor: Mark A. Aho
- Relationship Manager: Sally Brown
- CPA: Mary Beth Stone
- Attorney: Frank Jones

Family Members' Names

1. Sarah, daughter
2. Philip, son

Value/Goals and Personal Objectives

1. Retire in the Upper Peninsula of Michigan
2. Build their dream home
3. Enjoy travel and vacations during retirement

Interests

1. They both enjoy reading
2. Hiking throughout areas of the UP
3. Travel
4. John enjoys golf, and Sandy likes to run outside and cross-country ski in the winter

Overall Purpose: "The purpose of the portfolio is to build funds for retirement and also a legacy pool of investments for our heirs and favorite charities. During our retirement years it is our goal to obtain income from the portfolio and to increase the income on an annual basis at or above the rate of inflation. At our death it is our goal to have a worthy legacy amount for our heirs and our favorite charities."

Investment Objectives

To meet its needs, the investment strategy of John and Sandy Grey is to emphasize total return: that is, the aggregate return from capital appreciation and dividend and interest income. Specifically, the primary objective in the investment management for investment account assets shall be: **Balanced/ Growth.** The primary objective is capital appreciation with some income through investment in equity and fixed income instruments. This overall portfolio will consist primarily of large capitalization and small capitalization equity issues (U.S., developed international, emerging markets will be represented most of the time); may also be invested in alternative investments; will also be invested in fixed income; will be diversified in both sector and security; may experience moderate losses through a market cycle.

Investment Time Horizon

The Investment Time Horizon is the amount of time from today during which it is expected that the majority of the investable assets will remain in this portfolio. If a substantial portion of the portfolio were expected to be liquidated, the investment time horizon would be the number of years until that event. Because John and Sandy Grey's investment portfolio represents a long-term time commitment for future use of the total return from these investments, the investment time horizon is ten-plus years.

Planned Deposits to Investments

- John and Sandy 401(k) deposits, $26,000 each
- HSA deposit of $5,100.

Need for Liquidity

There is no specific liquidity need at this time.

Need for Income

There is no need for income from this portfolio at this time.

Risk Tolerance

Risk tolerance can best be described as moderate. Willing to accept some risk for an average return on investments. Subject to ongoing monitoring and periodic review, interim fluctuations in market value and rates of return may be tolerated in order to achieve longer-term objectives.

Performance Expectations

The long term expectations for investment portfolio return will be measured on a total return basis. The total expected average return is: See goal plan in Appendix B.

Performance Review and Evaluation

Total performance relative to objectives and individual manager performance will be reviewed semi-annually and evaluated relative to objectives over a three- to five-year market cycle. Investment managers shall be reviewed regarding performance, personnel, strategy, research capabilities, organizational and business matters, and other qualitative factors that may impact their ability to achieve the desired investment results.

Tax Bracket

John and Sandy Grey currently file a joint tax return and are currently in the 22% marginal Federal income tax bracket.

Investment Portfolio Asset Allocation Overview

Asset Class:	Minimum	Preferred	Maximum
• Cash	1%	1%	20%
• Bonds	10%	29%	50%
• Stocks	50%	70%	90%

*Generally, no more than a 10 percent deviation from the preferred allocation is targeted.

Tax-Deferred 401(k)/IRAs
Strategic Asset Allocation by Asset Class
Asset Class Preferred Exposure

Asset Class	Exposure
• U.S. Large Cap Growth Stocks	13%
• U.S. Large Cap Value Stocks	13%
• U.S. Small Cap Growth Stocks	13%
• U.S. Small Cap Value Stocks	13%
• Dev. International/Emerging Markets*	15%
• Global Real Estate-REIT	3%
• U.S. Government/Corporate Bonds	18%
○ Short-Intermediate Duration/High Quality	
• Global Bonds	11%
• Cash	1%
Total	100%

*Assigned manager will determine allocation towards Developed International and Emerging Market and monitored internally by MAFG.

Taxable Investment Portfolio
Strategic Asset Allocation by Asset Class
Asset Class Preferred Exposure

Asset Class	Exposure
• U.S. Large Capitalization Stocks*	50%
• U.S. Fixed Income Municipal Tax Free	30%
○ Short-Intermediate Duration/High Quality	
• U.S. Small Cap Growth	5%
• U.S. Small Cap Value	5%
• Dev. International/Emerging Markets	10%
Total	100%

*The portfolio will primarily consist of high quality U.S. large capitalization companies with a global reach. This portfolio is managed on the basis of companies paying and growing their dividends paid to investors. The intent is to have a well-diversified portfolio of at least twenty-five companies in at least five of the eleven S&P sectors. The overall intent of this portfolio is to be invested in high quality companies paying a current and consistently growing dividend.

Rebalancing to Desired Strategy

From time to time, market conditions will cause your portfolio's investments to vary from the original allocation we established. To remain consistent with the overall guidelines established in this Investment Policy statement, each security in which the portfolio is invested may be reviewed at intervals and rebalanced back to the normal weighting.

The financial representative will determine the review interval and the amount of variance allowed in an attempt to balance the goals of proper allocation vs. minimizing transaction costs and fees.

Financial Assets Currently Held at Raymond James

Date	Total Assets
7/13/2021	$1,750,000

The aggregate fee on your accounts is (are): .96 bps

Financial Assets Retirement/Wealth Building Plan (See Goal Plan)

Estate Planning

- Will completed and reviewed March, 2018
- Executor: Themselves
- Power of Attorney: Sarah
- Power of Health: Philip

- Trust completed and reviewed March 2018
- Successor Trustee: Sarah

Insurance

- Long-Term Care: yes—purchased a ten-year payment policy with Nationwide
- Umbrella Coverage: yes—$3 million with their insurance agent
- Health Savings Account (HSAs)—Start this year with $5,100
- Life Insurance: None

Executor/Trustee Issues

Gifting

No gifting is in the foreseeable future. This will be revisited.

Business Succession Plans Issues

None.

Duties and Responsibilities

The financial representative is responsible to assist the investor in making an appropriate asset allocation decision based on the particular needs, objectives, and risk tolerance of the investor. The financial representative will be available on a regular basis to meet with the investor and review the portfolio based on information provided by the investor.

The investor is responsible to provide the financial representative with all relevant and accurate information on financial condition, net worth, and risk tolerances and must promptly notify the advisor of any changes to this information.

Recommendations

All of our recommendations will be made in conjunction with this PFPS and Goal Plan. This will ensure that the strategies we choose will be consistent with your goals, objectives, and priorities. At times we may make recommendations that we feel are essential to your family's well-being and security, even though these recommendations may not be directly related to issues we have discussed. Nonetheless, all of our recommendations will follow directly from this document and will be in your best interest.

Our Service—Updates and Reviews

- Personal Meetings—Comprehensive Semi-Annual Review
- Process—How involved do you like to be in managing your finances?
- Preferred method of contact—Email/Phone/Letter

Basically on an as needed basis by the advisor or the client, however, the advisor service team may call you in the quarter which there was no personal review meeting. We will be available at your convenience and we will make every effort possible to return all messages within twenty hours. We expect the same consideration from you.

- Reporting
  - Investment Statements Monthly or Quarterly by Account type
  - Performance Reports: Quarterly by account type
  - Tax reporting: Annually
  - PFPS updates: Annually or as required
  - Goal Plan updates: Semi-Annual Review

- Publications: Newsletter—Quarterly
- Website and advisor access: MarkAhoFinancial.com

Investment Policy Review

Your Financial Advisor will review this Investment Policy Statement (IPS) and your Goal Plan with you at least annually to determine whether stated investment objectives are still relevant. It is not expected that the IPS will change frequently. In particular, short-term changes in the financial markets should not require adjustments to the IPS. It is the obligation of the Client to notify all interested parties of any material changes that would alter the objectives or construction of this portfolio. If all interested parties are not notified of these material changes, then the current investment policy is invalid.

This IPS is not a contractual agreement of any kind and therefore by signing it you will not be bound to any arrangement. It is only meant to be a summary of the agreed upon investment management techniques.

See the complete Personal Financial Policy Statement in Appendix C.

❧ ❧ ❧ ❧ ❧

As you review your own Personal Financial Policy Statement each year, note that your overall financial goals and objectives do not change. Your financial advisor will suggest tweaks to accomplish the retirement you desire and so that you can answer the four basic questions in the affirmative.

Often we fall prey to the fallacy that our long-term goal cannot be met because we haven't accomplished everything according to the original plan. Not true. The goal remains the same. The path to get there adjusts to make it happen.

Now it's your turn to build your Personal Financial Policy Statement. You've got the basic tools and information to put this information together.

If you, like John and Sandy, look at your long-term financial goals and discover some gaps, don't give up. Your future remains bright and hopeful. Schedule a meeting with your financial advisor.

Achieve Your Dream—Action Step

Build your Personal Financial Policy Statement in Appendix C.

10

WHEN DO YOU REACH ENOUGH?

Knowing is not enough; we must apply.
Willing is not enough; we must do.

—Johann Wolfgang Von Goethe

Now that you've completed the Personal Financial Policy Statement, it's time to identify your next steps.

The first question every person asks is, "Do I have enough?" By this point, you have a good idea of what you want, your needs, and your future plans. If you haven't taken the time to complete the Achieve Your Dream – Action Step questions at the end of the first five chapters, stop and do that now. It will help you move through this next section.

Enough. What a difficult word to define. For one person, enough might mean a solid bank account, money leftover at the end of the month, and a two-week vacation every year. But to someone else it could mean one million in investments by the time they're thirty-five, a 5,000 square-foot home on the waterfront somewhere, a Tesla, and European vacations four times a year.

The flipside of enough is the lack of wealth or even poverty. Wess Stafford, former president of Compassion International, says, "The opposite of poverty is not wealth. It is enough."[1] According to Credit Suisse, if you live in the United States, even at the lower end of the economic ladder, you live in the country that controls almost 30 percent of the world's wealth[2]. As such, you have a higher net worth than anybody else in the world.

Having *enough* is a personal measure, and as I mentioned earlier in this book, enough is not only about wealth; answering the *enough* question requires more than financial numbers. Enough is a mindset as much as it is a number in your bank account. Whether or not you have enough depends on you.

Remember: your mindset determines how you approach your life. A fixed mindset believes that life is the way it is and is impossible to influence or change. *Que sera sera* or what will be will be is the personal theme of a person with a fixed mindset. But a growth mindset believes that it is possible to grow, change, reach higher, and push farther than one's current circumstances. Will you always succeed in reaching your goals? Probably not. But the effort it takes to reach a goal just beyond your reach always results in challenge and growth. You will discover more in that stretching than in being satisfied with the way things are.

Carol Dweck offers this thought that I believe is helpful in considering the *enough* question: "No matter what your ability is, effort is what ignites that ability and turns it into accomplishment." Dweck challenges us to stretch ourselves and stick to the path we've decided to pursue especially when it's not going well. Staying the course and putting a concerted effort toward your goal is the hallmark of the growth mindset because it allows you to thrive during your most trying or difficult seasons of life.

As a family steward you must embody a growth mindset. Your definition of enough must focus on the future, not the present. A family steward cares more about leaving a deep legacy of faith, joy, and belief. If there are some funds to pass along upon death, even better.

As you process this question, "Do I have enough?" check your mindset. Would your best friend describe your mindset as fixed or growth? Talk with your spouse about your current life. Do you have enough? What does *enough* mean to you? What will *enough* look like?

The second part of this question deals with how to know you have enough. Again, the answer varies for each person, couple, and family. But as you look at your personal financial goals, you will get a good idea of where you stand because you have a target in mind.

Looking Toward the Future

If you choose to spend every dollar you earn without a thought for future needs, where does that leave you? In this case, you'd probably believe you didn't have enough. But, if your best friend earns a similar income, invests portions of that income, and lives on less than he takes home each paycheck, he probably believes he has enough. If you always look at the bottom line or your bank account balance as your determiner for having enough, you will never answer this question positively. You continually search for more.

Is it wrong to search for ways to increase your bottom line? Of course not. But *enough* isn't a question of increasing your bottom line. You must know what *enough* means to you before you can determine if you've met it. Chasing an elusive number won't tell you if you've reached *enough*.

You need a written plan. You, and your spouse if you are married, must explore what *enough* looks like *for you*. Write down your goal(s). Describe it so you know when you reach it. Then, you compare your plan with your current reality. If there are gaps—and there probably will be—consider how you can cover the gaps. Do you need to work a second job? Find a higher paying job? Are there items in your current spending pattern that could be eliminated temporarily to ease the budget?

Keep focused on your ultimate goal. Refer to your personal financial plan. The truth is you can reach your goal if you determine to do that. Earlier I told you about the house we bought and eventually sold because it was too much of a strain on our budget. Living in the smaller home at that time moved us from over-extended into *enough*. Having faith in the future, we knew that our decisions at that time would affect our future positively. And they did. We had and still have *enough*. Because we clearly defined our *enough* and designed our life to fulfill that vision.

ACHIEVE YOUR DREAM—ACTION STEP

Write out what enough *means to you, your spouse, and your family. Be specific. Remember, clarity allows you to plan well and execute the plan.*

11
MORE THAN ENOUGH

Financial freedom is available to those who learn about it and work for it.

—Robert Kiyosaki

Now that you've defined *enough* for your life and family, it's time to move on to the next question every person asks: "Can I live the life I want to live?"

Before you can answer that question, you must have a description of that life.

"Can I do what I want?" is a loaded question. If you are married, perhaps the better question to ask is, "Can we do what brings us joy?"

Often, when we set out to do what we want, we find it a very selfish lifestyle. It doesn't have to be that way though. Several people who have more than enough practice wonderful generosity. Their goal isn't to increase their wealth for their bottom line, but to use that increase to provide for and bless others.

To John and Sandy Grey, part of their present and future *enough* is enjoying new experiences. Their current lifestyle affords them many new experiences. And, because they've done yearly evaluations of their financial plan, they feel confident that this option will continue. At their last meeting with their financial advisor, they reviewed their Financial Goal Plan in detail.

When John and Sandy talked with their financial advisor who took them back through the six guiding principles of investing, they realized they were in a good financial position. A few simple tweaks were all that was needed. They discussed the purpose of their half-time adjustment once again. The team doesn't make major strategy changes. They simply refined the current plan to better achieve their goals.

As John and Sandy accept their adjusted retirement date to allow for a larger portfolio before entering retirement, they feel confident this is a wise decision. They know that putting additional funds into their retirement accounts now allows for more flexibility for new experiences in the future. At their current level of savings, they come up a bit short. John and Sandy know they want to have enough to travel, be generous with their kids, grandkids, and charitable organizations. Their more-than-enough mindset is motivated by a heart of generosity.

WHAT DO YOU TREASURE?

This concept of "more than enough" goes back to our understanding of biblical abundance. The Bible talks about money, wealth, and possessions more than 2,000 times. Jesus spoke often about money as well. Why? Because He knows money is a heart issue. In Matthew 6:19–21, Jesus says, "Don't store up treasures here on earth, where moths eat them and rust destroys them, and where thieves break in and steal. Store your treasures in heaven, where moths and rust cannot destroy, and thieves do not break in and steal. Wherever your treasure is, there the desires of your heart will also be" (NLT).

What do you treasure? What is highly precious to you? Jesus says in these verses to check our heart about our treasures. Are they such that will last for eternity, or could they be eaten by moths, destroyed by fire or rust, or stolen by another person?

When I consider my greatest treasures, they are my wife, family, friends, values, and legacy. No one can take those from me. As a family steward, I put my energies into caring for those people and things. I know that building important relationships has eternal value.

Money Is a Means of Exchange, Not Treasure

In the United States, dollar bills used to be backed by silver. Years ago, bills had the words "Silver Certificate"[1] on them to indicate this piece of paper was redeemable for silver. This method gave investors the ability to hold this precious metal without actually buying it. Once the federal government stopped printing these notes, their value dropped.

Also of interest is the gold standard.[2] There is a long history of how gold backed our currency. In August of 1971, however, President Nixon severed the direct convertibility of U.S. dollars into gold. With this decision, the international currency market, which had become increasingly reliant on the dollar since the enactment of the Bretton Woods Agreement, lost its formal connection to gold. The U.S. dollar, and by extension, the Global financial system it effectively sustained, entered the era of fiat money[3]. The value of fiat money derives from the relationship between supply and demand and the stability of the issuing government, rather than the worth of a commodity backing it.

Currently, our money's value is determined by the government (fiat money). The same is true for other countries. Its value changes with the whims of the government, which is why I say it is only a means of exchange. Money's main use involves how we use it and what methods we use to obtain it. When I talk about building wealth, money is one component.

True wealth involves building a holistic legacy. Therefore, answering the question about enough or building more than enough requires an honest evaluation of one's entire life. What is my motivation for all I choose to do and my future goals? Earning money for money's sake feels empty and unfulfilling. But building wealth to provide for my family and to serve others well excites me.

Seneca, a Roman philosopher, statesman, and orator from the mid-first century said, "It's not the man who has too little, but the man who craves more, that is poor." Do you crave money for money's sake? Check your heart attitude toward finances and abundance.

Mother Theresa, a well-known figure within the Catholic church and the world at large, knew what it meant to live with the poorest of the poor. In pure financial terms, she was not wealthy. When you look at the totality of her life, however, she had great wealth and built great wealth, the treasures that cannot be destroyed.

Do you believe in biblical abundance? How do you know you have biblical abundance? It's time to answer this question.

If you haven't reviewed your financial plan in the last year, now is a good time to schedule that review. You cannot know if you have more than enough if you haven't defined enough for your lifestyle, dreams, and desires.

Achieve Your Dream—Action Step

What brings you joy?

How would you define more than enough for your lifestyle and retirement?

What adjustments might you need to make to achieve these goals?

Take time to write them out. Be specific.

12
ENOUGH TO GIVE

We make a living by what we get. We make a life by what we give.

—Winston Churchill

In Jim Stovall's book, *The Ultimate Gift,* we enter the story about a gentleman who'd done quite well throughout his lifetime. Unfortunately, as with many families, spats arose causing divisions within his family. Upon this gentleman's death and the reading of the will, the lawyer informed the family members that once they learned about their inheritance, they must leave the room. No exceptions. The lawyer read the preamble to the will which stated that all family members must be present while the will was read.

While the lawyer dispassionately read the terms of the will, several family members, who believed it was their right to inherit larger portions of the estate than what they were bequeathed, threatened to sue the estate and the beneficiary. Each left with a parting shot at the lawyer until one person remained. Stunned, the final family member hears the terms of his inheritance.

As the story unfolds, this entitled and rather spoiled family member discovers the true meaning of wealth, wisdom, and philanthropy. But first, the young person loses everything he'd been accustomed to in recent years. Penniless and homeless, his life lessons begin. At any juncture in this process, he can lose it all if he doesn't meet every condition of the will. The beneficiary discovers that life is more than enjoying yourself and doing what you want. When the final inheritance is received, which was more than anyone knew, this family member discovered what the grandfather knew. Money is a tool to be used to meet your needs and serve others well.

The grandfather in this story desired his grandchild learn early in life what took the grandfather many years to discover. The richest person on earth is the one who loves well and serves his fellow human being with joy. People matter most.[1]

Every family steward I've ever met understands this principle. That's why this question, *Can I help others?* is so important to them.

CAN I HELP OTHERS?

Each person considers this question differently. How you answer will depend on your financial goals. So, let's look back to your personal financial plan. What did you identify as important? Does it include an aspect of helping others?

For the person who wants to spend what they earn and not leave anything behind upon their passing, the answer to this question looks different than it does someone with a different perspective on legacy.

Some people might set aside a certain percentage of their income to contribute during their lifetime to specific causes. They are generous with what they have, but may or may not consider it important to have this philanthropic activity extend after their death.

Other people may not have the resources to help others financially, but offer assistance through volunteering and mentoring. Their generosity involves devoting time and energy to causes.

A family steward may also be concerned about how much financial resources to leave to a family member and the timing of the gift. Often you hear of children or grandchildren who inherit a large sum of money without the training or wisdom to manage those funds well. Instead, they develop an entitlement attitude, which causes other issues. For this steward, the legacy is as much about money as it is about character development.

Who's to say what enriches lives more—the financial resources or the personal investment? Both have value and purpose.

How Do You Know if You Can Help Others?

As a family steward, you must answer this question through a legacy lens. It necessitates both a financial and personal component. And, if both avenues cannot be funded, you may believe you have failed to answer this question well.

The first way you discover this answer is to live on less than you make. When you achieve this status, you have available funds to disperse as you desire. But what about the person who continues to live paycheck to paycheck? How do they help others?

Many great philanthropic organizations crave volunteers. If you have more time than money at this point in your life, look for places and people to whom you can invest your time, energy, and experience. Here are a few places to consider that may need your help:

- Schools often need tutors or readers to help in classrooms or after-school options. Check your local school district for information.

- Churches are another great way to volunteer your time and energy.
- Hospitals and health care centers, hospice, and homeless shelters are great places to help others.
- Community service organizations like Kiwanis, Boys & Girls Clubs, Scouting programs, your local library, and business economic assistance groups often need volunteers for any number of roles.

As you can see, many options exist depending on your talents, abilities, and interests. Helping others doesn't have to involve money. Your presence and assistance may be more valuable than any amount of financial resources you could donate.

If you are able to live on less than you earn, consider how you want to use those extra funds to serve others. If you are married, having this discussion is key. One person should not make the decision for the other.

My wife and I support several organizations with our funds. We chose these groups based on our beliefs and the organization's focus or community impact. We routinely evaluate our support of these groups and consider other options as well. The Bible says that God loves a cheerful giver.[2] Jesus highlighted a woman who gave two pennies over others who gave much more because the woman gave her funds out of love for God. This passage reminds me to check my motivation each time I give. Am I cheerful and giving because it is a joy to share the blessings God has given me?

Do you see how helping others is more than writing a check? How does this idea fit within your definition of helping others? Defining an abundant life requires a holistic approach.

Now it's your turn to answer this question for yourself.

ACHIEVE YOUR DREAM—ACTION STEP

Set aside thirty minutes minimum to answer the question we discussed in this chapter. If you are married, discuss this question with your spouse.

Can you help others? Why or why not?

What are you doing today to help others?

What more could you do?

How will you do it?

13

ENOUGH FOR LASTING IMPACT

The greatest legacy one can pass on to one's children and grandchildren is not money . . . but rather a legacy of character and faith.

—Billy Graham

Stephen Covey said to begin with the end in mind. With that sound advice in mind, we must ask the fourth and final question: "Can I impact the next generation and those to come?"

I encourage every person I work with to ask the four financial questions because if we want to begin with the end in mind, we need the answers to these questions to direct our plans and actions. As I meet with clients quarterly and annually to review their personal financial goals, investment strategies, Financial Goal Plan, and other documents, I show them how we can make necessary corrections and adjustments. My role as the financial advisor (coach) is to keep my eyes on their stated goal. Then to advise them about how to achieve those goals.

In the early stages of this financial planning process, we create a strategy with the end goal in mind. If we've done this work thoroughly together, my clients should be able to answer this question easily. If not, we have work to do.

One of my goals is to make this process as simple and easy to understand as possible. My hope is that as you've read this book and answered the questions for yourself, you've established plans—having contacted our offices or connected with another qualified financial advisor—to ensure that you can say without a doubt that your contribution to this world will outlive your time on it.

John and Sandy have reviewed their plan and made tweaks along the way.

After a recent meeting with their financial advisor, John and Sandy felt at peace knowing they could answer the first three questions well. They had consistently worked their plan and were seeing the results begin to take shape. On the drive home, however, John mentioned to Sandy that he felt a twinge of regret. Sandy listened thoughtfully as he pondered whether there was more they could have done. Probably. But more than once, life had interrupted their well-crafted plans. As Sandy and John continue to discuss the question of impact, they brainstorm ideas to further help them achieve their overall financial goals.

The next day, the Greys talked more about their recent meeting. John voiced his concern that they would leave a legacy for the next generation. At this point, he can't think beyond that. Throughout the next weeks and months, John and Sandy write down thoughts about how they can impact their grandchildren and future generations.

No one answers this question easily. In truth, it is difficult to understand the true implications of this question until you get closer to the end of life.

Through the years of working with many clients, I've seen how creating a solid financial plan works *and* helps answer this last question before clients are even ready to consider it for themselves. Family stewards live on less, invest and save wisely, and are generous. It is this lifestyle that allows them to invest in and impact future generations in both financial and personal ways.

Like wealth, legacy is more than money. Think about your core life values. How have you expressed these values?

Whether we want to admit it or not, who we are speaks loudly in how we live. We pass on these core values passively and actively. Think about an alcoholic or an addict. They pass on a legacy to their children. Children of alcoholics often inherit feelings of low self-esteem, fear of abandonment, need constant approval from others, and judge themselves harshly. They struggle to develop healthy personal relationships.

If you have a healthy nurturing marriage, your children inherit certain values. They probably see marriage as a blessing and highly valued, feel stable in who they are, and seek healthy relationships for themselves. Though not a guarantee, children who grow up in loving homes tend to view the world with more optimism and hope.

As you consider this question about your long-term impact, ask yourself what kind of legacy you wish to leave to your grandchildren and their children. Is it financial or some other kind of legacy? How will you accomplish it?

I call this the Legacy Road. Look at this simple illustration [see Figure 11]. When I work through this financial planning process with my clients, we discuss the various options. Some of my clients, the Family Stewards, spend more time and energy focusing on how to impact future generations. How can you use the accumulated wealth to bless others? You continue to build as much wealth as possible which provides you a good standard of living. But you also have faith in the future to invest a portion of your wealth to bless family members and even charities for generations to come.

But there is another path. You can choose to spend all your money, to enjoy the results of your hard work through the years, by the time you die. You have no desire to leave any form of financial legacy to future generations. Though you may leave a legacy in other areas such as work ethic, physical goods, humor, faith, and such. Some people might consider this the less greedy option because you created just enough wealth to take care of your needs.

Which one do you think is the path of greed versus wealth?

Figure 11: The Road to Greed

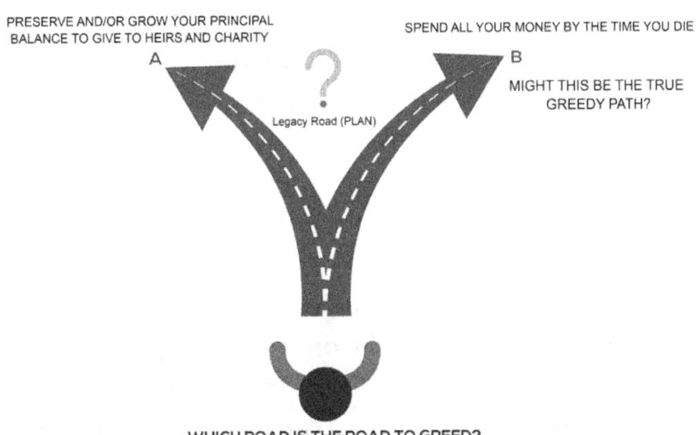

I argue that Path A allows you to build wealth and a future legacy that impacts others for generations to come. You determine to work hard, tithe, and grow as much wealth as possible. Not for lining your pockets, but for the well-being of future generations and people in need throughout the world. This road exemplifies your faith in the future, patience, and discipline. That's a legacy I can live with. How about you?

Two Options for Ensuring Financial Legacy

If you have the financial resources, you can work with a financial advisor and a lawyer to set up methods to distribute financial resources for your family and other philanthropic desires for generations to come.

Let's review some of these options for your consideration.

A Charitable Trust of Donor Advised Fund

Your financial legacy can be tied to your spiritual legacy. By creating a donor-advised fund (DAF), your generosity and dedication to contributing to the greater good of the human spirit can last for many generations. A DAF is a philanthropic endeavor you can establish that allows donors to make contributions at any time while receiving an immediate tax benefit for yourself. Subsequently, grants from the fund can be given to various charitable organizations by the trustees of the fund.

As the trustee of the DAF, you decide where the money goes, and it can be as much or as little as you like, as opposed to the charitable trust, where you have to donate 5 percent or more every year. You can also name who the successors of the DAF will be after you've passed. In other words, you can declare your children will be the ones who decide what money goes to which charity. When they're gone, they can name their children, and so on. In that way, your philanthropic spirit can live virtually forever!

The establishment of a charitable family trust or DAF can be very beneficial for mitigating taxes for two reasons:

1. **You can contribute to low-cost stocks:** You can contribute the shares of your low-cost stocks to your charitable trust or DAF and forego paying the capital gains tax, which could be fifteen or twenty percent.

2. **You can deduct the full value:** In most cases, the full value of the contribution can be a total deduction from your income. (It must satisfy the 30/50 percent rule.) If you are unable to deduct the full amount in the current tax year because of this rule, you can carry the remaining amount forward to deduct in a future year.

Compliance Note: Donors are urged to consult their attorneys, accountants or tax advisors with respect to questions relating to the deductibility of various types of contributions to a Donor-Advised Fund for federal and state tax purposes.

Qualified Charitable Distribution from an IRA

According to IRS.gov[1], a qualified charitable distribution is an otherwise taxable distribution from an IRA (other than an ongoing SEP or SIMPLE IRA) owned by an individual who is age seventy-and-a-half or older that is paid directly from the IRA to a qualified charity. Donations done this way satisfy part or all of the required minimum distributions for the IRA and reduce your income taxes. At the time of this writing, the maximum amount you can distribute annually is $100,000. Check with your financial advisor if this interests you as there are several factors to consider to set this up properly.

Evaluate Your Impact

Consider the most potent impact you may have on future generations has more to do with relationships than finances. Take the time and make the effort to be fully present and interested in the next generation. Get into their world, listen to their questions, be present, and pay attention.

Achieve Your Dream—Action Step

If you knew your life would end in the next twenty-four hours, how would you know you've impacted the next and future generations? Be specific.

If you don't know how to answer that question, brainstorm your desires and dreams here. Then, write down your first step to make this happen.

PART 5

Championship

14
LIVING THE CHAMPIONSHIP LIFE

Good judgment comes from experience,
and a lot of that comes from bad judgment.

—Will Rogers

Congratulations! You made it to the championship celebration because you took the time and energy to become a championship player. This is a great investment in itself.

How can you know you will be successful? Let's review the example in Matthew 25 of the Master and his servants. Two of the servants did well with what was entrusted to them. But one servant buried what he was given because he was afraid. Fear does that to us—it removes our options quickly.

To combat fear, we must remember the investment principle of having faith in the future. When you look at your life through the faith lens, you will see multiple opportunities and find satisfaction about what you do in your life.

Fear robs you of joy and faith. It limits your outlook and possibilities. Optimism is the only realism. There simply is no other way to think. Remind yourself and your heart each and every day to have faith in the future.

As the first two servants heard "well done" from the Master, they entered into a joyful existence. That probably sounds a little odd. But think of it this way. If you walk in faith throughout your life, you don't have any regrets. You've done everything you could to be a faithful family steward. No, you didn't do everything perfectly. You did your best. That's what a life of no regrets means. You live life fully, take appropriate risks, and care for your family the best you know how.

❦ ❦ ❦ ❦ ❦

John and Sandy Grey didn't do life perfectly. In fact, they look back at some of their earlier mistakes and shake their heads. Sure they wish they hadn't made them, but when reviewing their current status and looking into the future, they know that life is good. They planned well and worked hard to achieve their dreams as well as provide a lasting legacy for future generations. They're confident and hopeful for what comes next.

❦ ❦ ❦ ❦ ❦

You desire to be a championship player. To answer the four questions takes determination, patience, faith, and discipline. When you practice the traits of the family steward, you also act like an investor, one who believes in the future and works hard to achieve clear goals.

As I look back at my life and into the future, I desire most of all to leave my children and grandchildren with knowledge and wisdom about life. Because I approach all of life from a faith-based perspective, I believe God has gifted me with wonderful talents and abilities to be as successful as I can. My life contains more wonderful blessings than I have time to list.

Look at your life and take inventory of your unique gifts, talents, and abilities. Maybe you've been given great financial freedom or gifts of excess finances that you use to bless others insightfully and generously. Your faithful stewardship of these gifts can impact your family, friends, and others for generations to come.

Maybe you're like my Aunt Madelyn who never had much financially but poured her life into her family, including me, in multiple ways. Her legacy of kindness, a strong work ethic, and love for God continues to impact my life. How thrilling to relate to her how rich her legacy was. In my opinion, Aunt Madelyn could answer the question yes to the question, "Did I do enough?" with complete confidence. I wouldn't trade her legacy for anything else.

Each of us have different talents. Some earn a lot of money. Others have physical abilities to help others. Some do both. The important thing is to recognize your gifts and share them with the world around you. We need what you bring to this world, whether that is financial resources, spiritual insight, emotional intelligence, physical prowess, or creativity. You bring unique value.

So, before you toss this book to the side because you don't have abundant finances, take another look at the true meaning of legacy. Yes, money is a component. But I would argue the non-tangible gifts you give your children, grandchildren, and following generations of wisdom, faith, love, hope for the future, relationship, and many others have more value.

This is the life of abundance. And that's my desire for you.

APPENDICES

APPENDIX A

TOTAL CLIENT PROFILE INTERVIEW GUIDE

Values

- What's important to you about money?

- When you get to the end of your life, what values do you want to define your life?

Goals

- What are your personal goals or goals with your money?

- When you think about your money, what concerns, needs or feelings come to mind?

Relationships

- What family relationships are most important to you?

- What is your religious orientation? How important are your relationships with people associated with your religion?

- Would you describe yourself as an introvert or an extrovert?

- What schools did you go to? How important is your relationship with these schools?

Advisors

- Lawyer -
- Life Insurance agent -
- Accountant -

Process

- How involved do you like to be in managing your finances?*

- How Often would you like a review/contact and in what manner (phone, Email, mail)

Interests

- Do you follow sports? Which are your favorite teams?

- What are your favorite types of TV programs and movies?

- What do you read?

- Do you have health concerns or interests? What is your health program?

- What are your hobbies?

- What would an ideal weekend or vacation be?

- What pets do you have?

Source: Prince & Associates.

APPENDIX B
SAMPLE FINANCIAL GOAL PLAN

Financial Goal Plan

John and Sandy Grey

July 26, 2021

Prepared by:

Mark Aho

Raymond James
205 N Lakeshore Blvd
Ste B
Marquette, MI 49855-4369
(906) 226-0880 | MARK.AHO@RAYMONDJAMES.COM
http://markahofinancial.com

Table Of Contents

IMPORTANT DISCLOSURE INFORMATION

IMPORTANT: The projections or other information generated by Goal Planning & Monitoring regarding the likelihood of various investment outcomes are hypothetical in nature, do not reflect actual investment results, and are not guarantees of future results.

The return assumptions in Goal Planning & Monitoring are not reflective of any specific product, and do not include any fees or expenses that may be incurred by investing in specific products. The actual returns of a specific product may be more or less than the returns used in Goal Planning & Monitoring. It is not possible to directly invest in an index. Financial forecasts, rates of return, risk, inflation, and other assumptions may be used as the basis for illustrations. They should not be considered a guarantee of future performance or a guarantee of achieving overall financial objectives. Past performance is not a guarantee or a predictor of future results of either the indices or any particular investment.

Goal Planning & Monitoring results may vary with each use and over time.

Goal Planning & Monitoring Assumptions and Limitations

Information Provided by You

Information that you provided about your assets, financial goals, and personal situation are key assumptions for the calculations and projections in this Report. Please review the Report sections titled "Personal Information and Summary of Financial Goals", "Current Portfolio Allocation", and "Tax and Inflation Options" to verify the accuracy of these assumptions. If any of the assumptions are incorrect, you should notify your financial advisor. Even small changes in assumptions can have a substantial impact on the results shown in this Report. The information provided by you should be reviewed periodically and updated when either the information or your circumstances change.

All asset and net worth information included in this Report was provided by you or your designated agents, and is not a substitute for the information contained in the official account statements provided to you by custodians. The current asset data and values contained in those account statements should be used to update the asset information included in this Report, as necessary.

Assumptions and Limitations

Goal Planning & Monitoring offers several methods of calculating results, each of which provides one outcome from a wide range of possible outcomes. All results in this Report are hypothetical in nature, do not reflect actual investment results, and are not guarantees of future results. All results use simplifying assumptions that do not completely or accurately reflect your specific circumstances. No Plan or Report has the ability to accurately predict the future. As investment returns, inflation, taxes, and other economic conditions vary from the Goal Planning & Monitoring assumptions, your actual results will vary (perhaps significantly) from those presented in this Report.

All Goal Planning & Monitoring calculations use asset class returns, not returns of actual investments. The projected return assumptions used in this Report are estimates based on average annual returns for each asset class. The portfolio returns are calculated by weighting individual return assumptions for each asset class according to your portfolio allocation. The portfolio returns may have been modified by including adjustments to the total return and the inflation rate. The portfolio returns assume reinvestment of interest and dividends at net asset value without taxes, and also assume that the portfolio has been rebalanced to reflect the initial recommendation. No portfolio rebalancing costs, including taxes, if applicable, are deducted from the portfolio value. No portfolio allocation eliminates risk or guarantees investment results.

Goal Planning & Monitoring does not provide recommendations for any products or securities.

IMPORTANT DISCLOSURE INFORMATION

Asset Class Name	Projected Return Assumption	Projected Standard Deviation
Cash & Cash Alternatives	1.00%	2.00%
Cash & Cash Alternatives (Tax-Free)	1.00%	2.00%
Investment Grade Long Maturity Fixed Income	3.25%	9.63%
Investment Grade Long Maturity Fixed Income (Tax-Free)	3.25%	9.63%
Investment Grade Intermediate Maturity Fixed Inc	2.75%	5.27%
Investment Grade Intermediate Maturity Fixed Inc (Tax-Free)	2.75%	5.27%
Investment Grade Short Maturity Fixed Income	2.00%	4.49%
Investment Grade Short Maturity Fixed Income (Tax-Free)	2.00%	4.49%
Non-Investment Grade Fixed Income	4.65%	10.01%
Non-Investment Grade Fixed Income (Tax-Free)	4.65%	10.01%
Non-U.S. Fixed Income	3.58%	9.83%
Non-U.S. Fixed Income (Tax-Free)	3.58%	9.83%
Global Fixed Income Strategies	3.91%	6.50%
Global Fixed Income Strategies (Tax-Free)	3.91%	6.50%
Multi-Sector Fixed Income Strategies	5.48%	7.33%
Multi-Sector Fixed Income Strategies (Tax-Free)	5.48%	7.33%
Fixed Income Other	2.75%	4.98%
Fixed Income Other (Tax-Free)	2.75%	4.98%
U.S. Large Cap Blend	6.61%	18.03%

Asset Class Name	Projected Return Assumption	Projected Standard Deviation
U.S. Large Cap Blend (Tax-Free)	6.61%	18.03%
U.S. Large Cap Value	6.61%	18.03%
U.S. Large Cap Value (Tax-Free)	6.61%	18.03%
U.S. Large Cap Growth	6.61%	18.03%
U.S. Large Cap Growth (Tax-Free)	6.61%	18.03%
U.S. Mid Cap Equity	6.84%	19.64%
U.S. Mid Cap Equity (Tax-Free)	6.84%	19.64%
U.S. Small Cap Equity	7.07%	22.15%
Non-U.S. Developed Market Equity	6.64%	20.36%
Non-U.S. Developed Market Equity (Tax-Free)	6.64%	20.36%
Non-U.S. Emerging Market Equity	7.79%	26.54%
Non-U.S. Emerging Market Equity (Tax-Free)	7.79%	26.54%
Global Equity Strategies	6.83%	18.47%
Global Equity Strategies (Tax-Free)	6.83%	18.47%
Equity Sector Strategies	6.61%	18.03%
Equity Sector Strategies (Tax-Free)	6.61%	18.03%
Real Estate	6.50%	21.20%
Real Estate (Tax-Free)	6.50%	21.20%
Equity Other	6.68%	19.90%
Equity Other (Tax-Free)	6.68%	19.90%
Alternative Strategies	4.75%	7.27%
Alternative Strategies (Tax-Free)	4.75%	7.27%
Commodities	3.47%	17.28%

IMPORTANT DISCLOSURE INFORMATION

Asset Class Name	Projected Return Assumption	Projected Standard Deviation
Commodities (Tax-Free)	3.47%	17.28%
Private Market Strategies	9.13%	24.43%
Private Market Strategies (Tax-Free)	9.13%	24.43%
Allocation Strategies (Equity Weighted)	5.95%	13.42%
Allocation Strategies (Equity Weighted) (Tax-Free)	5.95%	13.42%
Allocation Strategies (Fixed Income Weighted)	4.79%	7.78%
Allocation Strategies (Fixed Income Weighted) (Tax-Free)	4.79%	7.78%
World Allocation Strategies	6.35%	9.97%
World Allocation Strategies (Tax-Free)	6.35%	9.97%
Conservative Strategies	3.94%	7.13%
Conservative Strategies (Tax-Free)	3.94%	7.13%
Moderate Conservative Strategies	4.66%	10.06%
Moderate Conservative Strategies (Tax-Free)	4.66%	10.06%
Moderate Strategies	5.42%	12.99%
Moderate Strategies (Tax-Free)	5.42%	12.99%
Moderate Aggressive Strategies	5.95%	15.42%
Moderate Aggressive Strategies (Tax-Free)	5.95%	15.42%

Goal Planning & Monitoring was developed by Raymond James in part using Mercer's Capital Markets Assumptions ("CMA") as a factor and includes such CMA in the report.

The CMA contains confidential and proprietary information of Mercer and is intended for the exclusive use of the parties to whom it was provided by Mercer. Its content may not be modified, sold or otherwise provided, in whole or in part, to any other person or entity without Mercer's prior written permission.

The findings, ratings and/or opinions expressed in the CMA are the intellectual property of Mercer and are subject to change without notice. They are not intended to convey any guarantees as to the future performance of the investment products, asset classes or capital markets discussed. Past performance is no guarantee of future results. Mercer's ratings do not constitute individualized investment advice.

The CMA does not contain investment advice relating to your particular circumstances. No investment decision should be made based on this information without first obtaining appropriate professional advice and considering your circumstances.

Information contained in the CMA may have been obtained from a range of third party sources. While the information is believed to be reliable, Mercer has not sought to verify it independently. As such, Mercer makes no representations or warranties as to the accuracy of the information presented and takes no responsibility or liability (including for indirect, consequential, or incidental damages) for any error, omission or inaccuracy in the data supplied by any third party.

The CMA does not constitute an offer to purchase or sell any securities, commodities, and/or any other financial instruments or products or constitute a solicitation on behalf of any of the investment managers, their affiliates, products or strategies that Mercer may evaluate or recommend.

For Mercer's conflict of interest disclosures, contact your Mercer representative or see www.mercer.com/conflictsofinterest.

Mercer does not provide tax or legal advice. You should contact your tax advisor, accountant and/or attorney before making any decisions with tax or legal implications.

Additional information on Mercer's methodology for CMA's can be provided by Raymond James upon request.

IMPORTANT DISCLOSURE INFORMATION

Risks Inherent in Investing

Investing in fixed income securities involves interest rate risk, credit risk, and inflation risk. Interest rate risk is the possibility that bond prices will decrease because of an interest rate increase. When interest rates rise, bond prices and the values of fixed income securities fall. When interest rates fall, bond prices and the values of fixed income securities rise. Credit risk is the risk that a company will not be able to pay its debts, including the interest on its bonds. This risk is higher with non-investment grade fixed income securities. Inflation risk is the possibility that the interest paid on an investment in bonds will be lower than the inflation rate, decreasing purchasing power.

Cash alternatives typically include money market securities and U.S. treasury bills. Investing in such cash alternatives involves inflation risk. In addition, investments in money market securities may involve credit risk and a risk of principal loss. Because money market securities are neither insured nor guaranteed by the Federal Deposit Insurance Corporation or any other government agency, there is no guarantee the value of your investment will be maintained at $1.00 per share. U.S. Treasury bills are subject to market risk if sold prior to maturity. Market risk is the possibility that the value, when sold, might be less than the purchase price.

Investing in stock securities involves volatility risk, market risk, business risk, and industry risk. The prices of most stocks fluctuate. Volatility risk is the chance that the value of a stock will fall. Market risk is chance that the prices of all stocks will fall due to conditions in the economic environment. Business risk is the chance that a specific company's stock will fall because of issues affecting it. Industry risk is the chance that a set of factors particular to an industry group will adversely affect stock prices within the industry. (See "Asset Class – Stocks" in the Glossary section of this Important Disclosure Information for a summary of the relative potential volatility of different types of stocks.)

International investing involves additional risks including, but not limited to, changes in currency exchange rates, differences in accounting and taxation policies, and political or economic instabilities that can increase or decrease returns.

Commodities are generally considered speculative because of the significant potential for investment loss. Commodities are volatile investments and should only form a small part of a diversified portfolio. There may be sharp price fluctuations even during periods when prices overall are rising.

Report Is a Snapshot and Does Not Provide Legal, Tax, or Accounting Advice

This Report provides a snapshot of your current financial position and can help you to focus on your financial resources and goals, and to create a plan of action. Because the results are calculated over many years, small changes can create large differences in future results. You should use this Report to help you focus on the factors that are most important to you. This Report does not provide legal, tax, or accounting advice. Before making decisions with legal, tax, or accounting ramifications, you should consult appropriate professionals for advice that is specific to your situation.

This information is provided for your convenience, but should not be used as a substitute for your account's monthly statements and trade confirmations. It has been gathered from information provided by you and other sources believed to be reliable.

Goal Planning & Monitoring Methodology

Goal Planning & Monitoring offers several methods of calculating results, each of which provides one outcome from a wide range of possible outcomes. The methods used are: "Average Returns," "Bad Timing," "Class Sensitivity," and "Monte Carlo Simulations."

Results Using Average Returns

The Results Using Average Returns are calculated using one average return for your pre-retirement period and one average return for your post-retirement period. Average Returns are a simplifying assumption. In the real world, investment returns can (and often do) vary widely from year to year and vary widely from a long-term average return.

Results with Bad Timing

Results with Bad Timing are calculated by using low returns in one or two years, and average returns for all remaining years of the Plan. For most Plans, the worst time for low returns is when you begin taking substantial withdrawals from your portfolio. The Results with Bad Timing assume that you earn a low return in the year(s) you select and then an Adjusted Average Return in all other years. This Adjusted Average Return is calculated so that the average return of the Results with Bad Timing is equal to the return(s) used in calculating the Results Using Average Returns. This allows you to compare two results with the same overall average return, where one (the Results with Bad Timing) has low returns in one or two years.

The default for the first year of low returns is two standard deviations less than the average return, and the default for the second year is one standard deviation less than the average return.

IMPORTANT DISCLOSURE INFORMATION

Results Using Class Sensitivity

The Results Using Class Sensitivity are calculated by using different return assumptions for one or more asset classes during the years you select. These results show how your Plan would be affected if the annual returns for one or more asset classes were different than the average returns for a specified period in your Plan.

Results Using Monte Carlo Simulations

Monte Carlo simulations are used to show how variations in rates of return each year can affect your results. A Monte Carlo simulation calculates the results of your Plan by running it many times, each time using a different sequence of returns. Some sequences of returns will give you better results, and some will give you worse results. These multiple trials provide a range of possible results, some successful (you would have met all your goals) and some unsuccessful (you would not have met all your goals). The percentage of trials that were successful is the probability that your Plan, with all its underlying assumptions, could be successful. In Goal Planning & Monitoring, this is the Probability of Success. Analogously, the percentage of trials that were unsuccessful is the Probability of Failure. The Results Using Monte Carlo Simulations indicate the likelihood that an event may occur as well as the likelihood that it may not occur. In analyzing this information, please note that the analysis does not take into account actual market conditions, which may severely affect the outcome of your goals over the long-term.

Goal Planning & Monitoring Presentation of Results

The Results Using Average Returns, Bad Timing, and Class Sensitivity display the results using an "Estimated % of Goal Funded" and a "Safety Margin."

Estimated % of Goal Funded

For each Goal, the "Estimated % of Goal Funded" is the sum of the assets used to fund the Goal divided by the sum of the Goal's expenses. All values are in current dollars. A result of 100% or more does not guarantee that you will reach a Goal, nor does a result under 100% guarantee that you will not. Rather, this information is meant to identify possible shortfalls in this Plan, and is not a guarantee that a certain percentage of your Goals will be funded. The percentage reflects a projection of the total cost of the Goal that was actually funded based upon all the assumptions that are included in this Plan, and assumes that you execute all aspects of the Plan as you have indicated.

Safety Margin

The Safety Margin is the estimated value of your assets at the end of this Plan, based on all the assumptions included in this Report. Only you can determine if that Safety Margin is sufficient for your needs.

Bear Market Loss and Bear Market Test

The Bear Market Loss shows how a portfolio would have been impacted during the worst bear market since the Great Depression. Depending on the composition of the portfolio, the worst bear market is either the "Great Recession" or the "Bond Bear Market."

The Great Recession, from November 2007 through February 2009, was the worst bear market for stocks since the Great Depression. In Goal Planning & Monitoring, the Great Recession Return is the rate of return, during the Great Recession, for a portfolio comprised of cash, bonds, stocks, and alternatives, with an asset mix equivalent to the portfolio referenced.

The Bond Bear Market, from July 1979 through February 1980, was the worst bear market for bonds since the Great Depression. In Goal Planning & Monitoring, the Bond Bear Market Return is the rate of return, for the Bond Bear Market period, for a portfolio comprised of cash, bonds, stocks, and alternatives, with an asset mix equivalent to the portfolio referenced.

The Bear Market Loss shows: 1) either the Great Recession Return or the Bond Bear Market Return, whichever is lower, and 2) the potential loss, if you had been invested in this cash-bond-stock-alternative portfolio during the period with the lower return. In general, most portfolios with a stock allocation of 20% or more have a lower Great Recession Return, and most portfolios with a combined cash and bond allocation of 80% or more have a lower Bond Bear Market Return.

The Bear Market Test, included in the Stress Tests, examines the impact on your Plan results if an identical Great Recession or Bond Bear Market, whichever would be worse, occurred this year. The Bear Market Test shows the likelihood that you could fund your Needs, Wants and Wishes after experiencing such an event.

IMPORTANT DISCLOSURE INFORMATION

Even though you are using projected returns for all other Goal Planning & Monitoring results, the Bear Market Loss and Bear Market Test use returns calculated from historical indices. These results are calculated using only three asset classes – Cash, Bonds, and Stocks. Alternative asset classes (e.g., real estate, commodities) are included in the Stocks asset class. The indices and the resulting returns for the Great Recession and the Bond Bear Market are:

Asset Class	Index	Great Recession Return 11/2007 – 02/2009	Bond Bear Market Return 07/1979 – 02/1980
Cash	Ibbotson U.S. 30-day Treasury Bills	2.31%	7.08%
Bond	Ibbotson Intermediate-Term Government Bonds – Total Return	15.61%	-8.89%
Stock	S&P 500 – Total Return	-50.95%	14.61%
Alternative	HFRI FOF: Diversified	-19.87%	N/A
	S&P GSCI Commodity - Total Return	N/A	23.21%

Notes

- HFRI FOF: Diversified stands for Hedge Fund Research Indices Fund of Funds
- S&P GSCI was formerly the Goldman Sachs Commodity Index

Because the Bear Market Loss and Bear Market Test use the returns from asset class indices rather than the returns of actual investments, they do not represent the performance for any specific portfolio, and are not a guarantee of minimum or maximum levels of losses or gains for any portfolio. The actual performance of your portfolio may differ substantially from those shown in the Great Recession Return, the Bond Bear Market Return, the Bear Market Loss, and the Bear Market Test.

Goal Planning & Monitoring Risk Assessment

The Goal Planning & Monitoring Risk Assessment highlights some – but not all – of the trade-offs you might consider when deciding how to invest your money. This approach does not provide a comprehensive, psychometrically-based, or scientifically-validated profile of your risk tolerance, loss tolerance, or risk capacity, and is provided for informational purposes only.

Based on your specific circumstances, you must decide the appropriate balance between potential risks and potential returns. Goal Planning & Monitoring does not and cannot adequately understand or assess the appropriate risk/return balance for you. Goal Planning & Monitoring requires you to select a risk score. Once selected, two important pieces of information are available to help you determine the appropriateness of your score: an appropriate portfolio for your score and the impact of a Bear Market Loss (either the Great Recession or the Bond Bear Market, whichever is lower) on this portfolio.

Goal Planning & Monitoring uses your risk score to select a risk-based portfolio on the Model Portfolio Table page. This risk-based portfolio selection is provided for informational purposes only, and you should consider it to be a starting point for conversations with your Advisor. It is your responsibility to select the Target Portfolio you want Goal Planning & Monitoring to use. The selection of your Target Portfolio, and other investment decisions, should be made by you, after discussions with your Advisor and, if needed, other financial and/or legal professionals.

Net Worth Detail - All Resources

This is your Net Worth Detail as of 07/26/2021. Your Net Worth is the difference between what you own (your Assets) and what you owe (your Liabilities). To get an accurate Net Worth statement, make certain all of your Assets and Liabilities are entered.

Description	John	Sandy	Joint	Total
Investment Assets				
Employer Retirement Plans				
401(k)	$850,000			$850,000
401(k)		$525,000		$525,000
Taxable and/or Tax-Free Accounts				
Taxable Investment Account			$375,000	$375,000
Total Investment Assets:	**$850,000**	**$525,000**	**$375,000**	**$1,750,000**
Other Assets				
Home and Personal Assets				
Home			$325,000	$325,000
Personal Property			$75,000	$75,000
Business and Property				
New home property			$70,000	$70,000
Texas Condo	$80,000			$80,000
Total Other Assets:	**$80,000**	**$0**	**$470,000**	**$550,000**
Net Worth:				**$2,300,000**

See Important Disclosure Information section in this Report for explanations of assumptions, limitations, methodologies, and a glossary.

Net Worth Summary - All Resources

This is your Net Worth Summary as of 07/26/2021. Your Net Worth is the difference between what you own (your Assets) and what you owe (your Liabilities). To get an accurate Net Worth statement, make certain all of your Assets and Liabilities are entered.

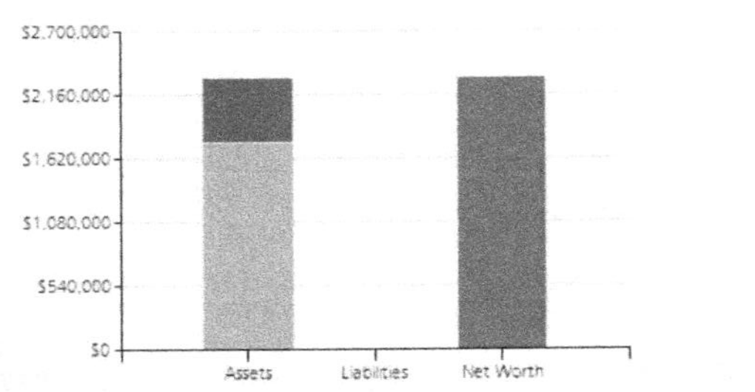

Investment Assets		$1,750,000
Other Assets	+	$550,000
Total Assets		$2,300,000
Total Liabilities	-	$0
Net Worth		$2,300,000

Description	Total
Investment Assets	
Employer Retirement Plans	$1,375,000
Taxable and/or Tax-Free Accounts	$375,000
Total Investment Assets:	**$1,750,000**
Other Assets	
Home and Personal Assets	$400,000
Business and Property	$150,000
Total Other Assets:	**$550,000**
Net Worth:	**$2,300,000**

See Important Disclosure Information section in this Report for explanations of assumptions, limitations, methodologies, and a glossary.

Current Portfolio Allocation

This page shows how your Investment Assets are currently allocated among the different Asset Classes. It includes only those Assets you have identified to fund Goals.

Total Stock
50%

Projected Returns

Total Return	4.25%
Base Inflation Rate	2.20%
Real Return	2.05%
Standard Deviation	9.24%

Bear Market Returns

Great Recession November 2007 thru February 2009	-19%
Bond Bear Market July 1979 thru February 1980	5%

Asset Class	Rate of Return	Investment Portfolio	
		Value	% of Total
Cash & Cash Alternatives	1.00%	$212,500	12.14%
Investment Grade Intermediate Maturity Fixed Inc	2.75%	$137,500	7.86%
Investment Grade Short Maturity Fixed Income	2.00%	$525,000	30.00%
U.S. Large Cap Blend	6.61%	$737,500	42.14%
U.S. Mid Cap Equity	6.84%	$68,750	3.93%
Non-U.S. Developed Market Equity	6.64%	$68,750	3.93%
	Total :	**$1,750,000**	**100%**

See Important Disclosure Information section in this Report for explanations of assumptions, limitations, methodologies, and a glossary.

Current Portfolio Allocation

Tax-Free Rates of Return	
Cash & Cash Alternatives	1.00%
Investment Grade Long Maturity Fixed Income	3.25%
Investment Grade Intermediate Maturity Fixed Inc	2.75%
Investment Grade Short Maturity Fixed Income	2.00%
Non-Investment Grade Fixed Income	4.65%
Non-U.S. Fixed Income	3.58%
Global Fixed Income Strategies	3.91%
Multi-Sector Fixed Income Strategies	5.48%
Fixed Income Other	2.75%
U.S. Large Cap Blend	6.61%
U.S. Large Cap Value	6.61%
U.S. Large Cap Growth	6.61%
U.S. Mid Cap Equity	6.84%
Non-U.S. Developed Market Equity	6.64%
Non-U.S. Emerging Market Equity	7.79%
Global Equity Strategies	6.83%
Equity Sector Strategies	6.61%
Real Estate	6.50%
Equity Other	6.68%
Alternative Strategies	4.75%
Commodities	3.47%
Private Market Strategies	9.13%
Allocation Strategies (Equity Weighted)	5.95%
Allocation Strategies (Fixed Income Weighted)	4.79%
World Allocation Strategies	6.35%
Conservative Strategies	3.94%
Moderate Conservative Strategies	4.66%

See Important Disclosure Information section in this Report for explanations of assumptions, limitations, methodologies, and a glossary.

Current Portfolio Allocation

Moderate Strategies	5.42%
Moderate Aggressive Strategies	5.95%

See Important Disclosure Information section in this Report for explanations of assumptions, limitations, methodologies, and a glossary.

Risk Assessment

You chose a Risk Score of 46.

Appropriate Portfolio: Balanced
Percentage Stock: 67%
Average Return: 5.45%

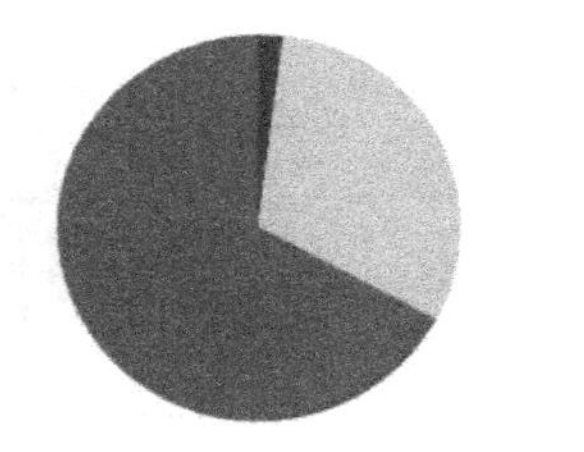

Great Recession Return Loss for this Portfolio

If this loss would cause you to sell your investments, you should select a lower score. Don't go past your Breaking Point.

During the Great Recession Return (November 2007 - February 2009) this portfolio had a loss of:

-29%

If you invest $1,750,000 in this portfolio and the same loss occurred again, you would lose:

-$511,896

See Important Disclosure Information section in this Report for explanations of assumptions, limitations, methodologies, and a glossary.

Model Portfolio Table

The Risk-Based Portfolio was selected from this list of Portfolios, based upon the risk assessment. The Risk Band is comprised of the portfolio(s) that could be appropriate for you, based upon the Risk-Based Portfolio indicated. The Target Portfolio was selected by you. Refer to the Standard Deviation column in the chart below to compare the relative risk of your Current Portfolio to the Target Portfolio.

Portfolios	Name	Cash	Bond	Stock	Alternative	Unclassified	Projected Return	Standard Deviation
	Conservative	2.00%	68.00%	30.00%	0.00%	0.00%	3.94%	7.01%
■	Current	12.14%	37.86%	50.00%	0.00%	0.00%	4.25%	9.24%
	Conservative Balanced	2.00%	48.00%	50.00%	0.00%	0.00%	4.76%	9.92%
	(c) AWS 60/40 2	1.00%	39.00%	60.00%	0.00%	0.00%	5.20%	11.69%
▼	Balanced	2.00%	31.00%	67.00%	0.00%	0.00%	5.45%	12.79%
▲	(c) AWS 70/30 3	1.00%	29.00%	70.00%	0.00%	0.00%	5.61%	13.46%
	Balanced w/ Growth	2.00%	15.00%	83.00%	0.00%	0.00%	6.08%	15.46%
	Growth	2.00%	0.00%	98.00%	0.00%	0.00%	6.62%	17.93%

Risk Band ■ Current ▼ Risk-Based ▲ Target

Return vs. Risk Graph

When deciding how to invest your money, you must determine the amount of risk you are willing to assume to pursue a desired return. The Return versus Risk Graph reflects a set of portfolios that assume a low relative level of risk for each level of return, or conversely an optimal return for the degree of investment risk taken. The graph also shows the position of the Risk Band, Target, Risk-Based, and Custom Portfolios. The positioning of these portfolios illustrates how their respective risks and returns compare to each other as well as the optimized level of risk and return represented by the Portfolios.

This graph shows the relationship of return and risk for each Portfolio in the chart above.

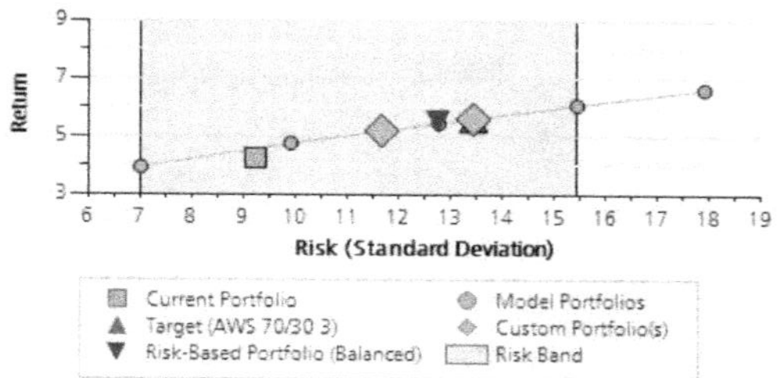

See Important Disclosure Information section in this Report for explanations of assumptions, limitations, methodologies, and a glossary.

What If Worksheet

This Worksheet allows you to analyze and compare the results of one or more scenarios that you created by varying the Plan assumptions.

	Estimated % of Goal Funded			
Goals	**Current Scenario**		**What If 1**	
	Average Return	Bad Timing	Average Return	Bad Timing
Need	100%	99%	100%	100%
10 Basic Living Expense				
10 Health Care				
Want	37%	0%	100%	100%
7 Travel				
7 New Retirement Home				
7 Car / Truck John				
7 Car / Truck Sandy				
Safety Margin (Value at End of Plan)				
Current dollars (in thousands) :	$0	$0	$1,610	$878
Future dollars (in thousands) :	$0	$0	$3,525	$1,921

Monte Carlo Results	Likelihood of Funding All Goals	
Your Confidence Zone: 75% - 90%	34% Probability of Success Below Confidence Zone	84% Probability of Success In Confidence Zone
Total Spending :	$4,257,201	$3,745,963

• Indicates different data between the Scenario in the first column and the Scenario in any other column.

See Important Disclosure Information section in this Report for explanations of assumptions, limitations, methodologies, and a glossary.

What If Worksheet

Key Assumptions	Current Scenario		What If 1
Stress Tests			
Method(s)	Bad Timing Program Estimate Years of bad returns: 2024: -18.16% 2025: -6.97%		Bad Timing Program Estimate Years of bad returns: 2027: -23.72% 2028: -9.25%
Hypothetical Average Rate of Return			
Before Retirement :	Current	•	AWS 70/30 3
Entered Return :	N/A		N/A
Composite Return :	4.25%	•	5.61%
Composite Standard Deviation :	9.24%	•	13.46%
Total Return Adjustment :	0.00%		0.00%
Adjusted Real Return :	2.05%	•	3.41%
After Retirement :	Current	•	AWS 60/40 2
Entered Return :	N/A		N/A
Composite Return :	4.25%	•	5.20%
Composite Standard Deviation :	9.24%	•	11.69%
Total Return Adjustment :	0.00%		0.00%
Adjusted Real Return :	2.05%	•	3.00%
Base inflation rate :	2.20%		2.20%

• Indicates different data between the Scenario in the first column and the Scenario in any other column.

See Important Disclosure Information section in this Report for explanations of assumptions, limitations, methodologies, and a glossary.

What If Worksheet

Key Assumptions	Current Scenario		What If 1
Goals			
Basic Living Expense			
Retirement Age			
John	62	•	65
Sandy	61	•	64
Planning Age			
John	92		92
Sandy	94		94
One Retired			
John Retired and Sandy Employed	$88,000		$88,000
Sandy Retired and John Employed	$0		$0
Both Retired			
Both Retired	$100,000	•	$95,000
One Alone - Retired			
Sandy Alone Retired	$80,000		$80,000
John Alone Retired	$0		$0
One Alone - Employed			
John Alone Employed	$0		$0
Sandy Alone Employed	$0		$0
Health Care			
Percentage of costs to use :	100%		100%
Cost determined by Schedule :	See details		See details
Travel			
Year :	When both are retired		When both are retired
Cost :	$6,000		$6,000
Is recurring :	Yes		Yes
Years between occurrences :	1		1
Number of occurrences :	15		15
New Retirement Home			

• Indicates different data between the Scenario in the first column and the Scenario in any other column.

See Important Disclosure Information section in this Report for explanations of assumptions, limitations, methodologies, and a glossary.

What If Worksheet

Key Assumptions	Current Scenario		What If 1
Goals			
Year :	2027		2027
Cost :	$300,000		$300,000
Car / Truck John			
Year :	2025		2025
Cost :	$20,000		$20,000
Is recurring :	Yes		Yes
Years between occurrences :	7		7
Number of occurrences :	3		3
Car / Truck Sandy			
Year :	2024		2024
Cost :	$20,000		$20,000
Is recurring :	Yes		Yes
Years between occurrences :	7		7
Number of occurrences :	3		3
Retirement Income			
Social Security			
Select Social Security Strategy	Current		Current
John			
Filing Method :	Normal		Normal
Age to File Application :	67		67
Age Retirement Benefits begin :	67		67
First Year Benefit :	$35,362	•	$35,377
Sandy			
Filing Method :	Normal		Normal
Age to File Application :	67		67
Age Retirement Benefits begin :	67		67
First Year Benefit :	$31,763	•	$31,776
Reduce Benefits By :	0%		0%

• Indicates different data between the Scenario in the first column and the Scenario in any other column.

See Important Disclosure Information section in this Report for explanations of assumptions, limitations, methodologies, and a glossary.

What If Worksheet

Key Assumptions	Current Scenario	What If 1
Asset Additions		
401(k)	Maximum	Maximum
Roth:	N/A	N/A
Maximum contribution each year:	Yes	Yes
% Designated as Roth:	0.00%	0.00%
Plan addition amount:	$28,880	$28,880
Year additions begin:	2021	2021
John - Fund All Goals		
401(k)	Maximum	Maximum
Roth:	N/A	N/A
Maximum contribution each year:	Yes	Yes
% Designated as Roth:	0.00%	0.00%
Plan addition amount:	$28,220	$28,220
Year additions begin:	2021	2021
Sandy - Fund All Goals		
Extra Savings by Tax Category		
John's Qualified		$0
Sandy's Qualified		$0
John's Roth		$0
Sandy's Roth		$0
John's Tax-Deferred		$0
Sandy's Tax-Deferred		$0
Taxable		$0
Other Assets		
Home		
Include in Plan :	Yes	Yes
When received :	2027	2027
Amount of cash received :	$325,000	$325,000

• Indicates different data between the Scenario in the first column and the Scenario in any other column.

See Important Disclosure Information section in this Report for explanations of assumptions, limitations, methodologies, and a glossary.

What If Worksheet

Key Assumptions	Current Scenario	What If 1
Cash Reserve		
Include :		No
Your Goal Coverage		
Needs :		5
Wants :		3
Wishes :		1
Minimum Amount in Cash Reserve :		$0
Annual offset for Cash Reserve :		$0
Selected Allocation :		
Return :		
Standard Deviation :		
Aspirational Bucket		
Include :		No
Additional :		$0
Selected Allocation :		
Return :		
Standard Deviation :		
Tax Options		
Include Tax Penalties :	Yes	Yes
Change Tax Rate?	No	No
Year To Change :		
Change Tax Rate by this % (+ or -) :	0.00%	0.00%

• Indicates different data between the Scenario in the first column and the Scenario in any other column.

See Important Disclosure Information section in this Report for explanations of assumptions, limitations, methodologies, and a glossary.

Worksheet Detail - Combined Details

Scenario : What If 1 using Average Return

These pages provide a picture of how your Investment Portfolio may hypothetically perform over the life of this Plan. The graph shows the effect on the value of your Investment Portfolio for each year. The chart shows the detailed activities that increase and decrease your Investment Portfolio value each year including the funds needed to pay for each of your Goals. Shortfalls that occur in a particular year are denoted with an 'X' under the Goal column.

Total Portfolio Value Graph

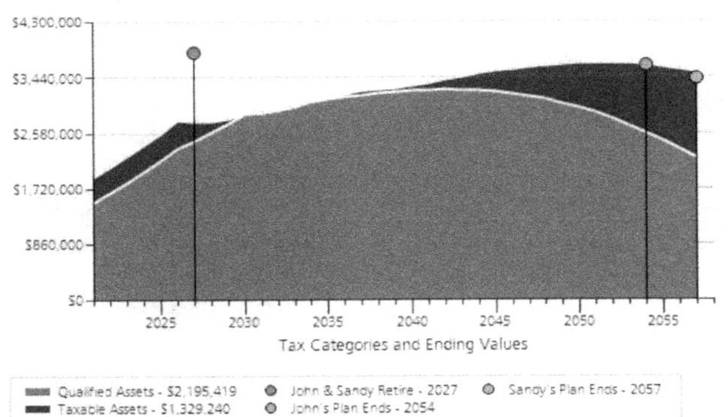

x - denotes shortfall

See Important Disclosure Information section in this Report for explanations of assumptions, limitations, methodologies, and a glossary.

Worksheet Detail - Combined Details

Scenario : What If 1 using Average Return

		Beginning Portfolio Value								Funds Used	
Event or Ages	Year	Earmarked	Fund All Goals	Additions To Assets	Other Additions	Post Retirement Income	Investment Earnings	Investment Return	Taxes	All Goals	Ending Portfolio Value
59/58	2021	0	1,750,000	57,100	0	0	101,433	5.61%	5,231	0	1,903,302
60/59	2022	0	1,903,302	57,212	0	0	110,044	5.61%	5,451	0	2,065,107
61/60	2023	0	2,065,107	58,327	0	0	119,188	5.61%	5,681	0	2,236,940
62/61	2024	0	2,236,940	59,444	0	0	127,698	5.61%	5,623	21,349	2,397,110
63/62	2025	0	2,397,110	61,564	0	0	136,781	5.61%	5,556	21,819	2,568,080
64/63	2026	0	2,568,080	62,686	0	0	147,665	5.61%	5,790	0	2,772,640
John & Sandy Retire	2027	0	2,772,640	0	325,000	0	136,373	5.21%	155	479,824	2,754,033
66/65	2028	0	2,754,033	0	0	0	136,651	5.21%	0	130,880	2,759,804
67/66	2029	0	2,759,804	0	0	42,105	138,870	5.21%	2,333	134,305	2,804,140
68/67	2030	0	2,804,140	0	0	81,682	142,268	5.21%	17,045	137,875	2,873,170
69/68	2031	0	2,873,170	0	0	83,479	143,827	5.21%	29,279	166,458	2,904,739
70/69	2032	0	2,904,739	0	0	85,315	145,279	5.21%	30,386	170,874	2,934,074
71/70	2033	0	2,934,074	0	0	87,192	148,451	5.21%	22,101	149,480	2,998,136
72/71	2034	0	2,998,136	0	0	89,110	151,631	5.21%	22,896	153,637	3,062,344
73/72	2035	0	3,062,344	0	0	91,071	154,493	5.21%	30,043	157,926	3,119,939
74/73	2036	0	3,119,939	0	0	93,074	157,290	5.21%	31,798	162,350	3,176,154
75/74	2037	0	3,176,154	0	0	95,122	160,006	5.21%	33,646	166,916	3,230,720
76/75	2038	0	3,230,720	0	0	97,215	161,121	5.21%	35,164	200,587	3,253,304
77/76	2039	0	3,253,304	0	0	99,353	162,041	5.21%	36,677	206,100	3,271,922
78/77	2040	0	3,271,922	0	0	101,539	164,320	5.21%	38,672	181,531	3,317,579
79/78	2041	0	3,317,579	0	0	103,773	166,452	5.21%	40,854	186,701	3,360,250
80/79	2042	0	3,360,250	0	0	106,056	168,913	5.21%	43,277	182,573	3,409,370
81/80	2043	0	3,409,370	0	0	108,389	171,222	5.21%	45,706	187,888	3,455,387
82/81	2044	0	3,455,387	0	0	110,774	173,359	5.21%	48,278	193,379	3,497,863
83/82	2045	0	3,497,863	0	0	113,211	175,304	5.21%	50,942	199,007	3,536,430
84/83	2046	0	3,536,430	0	0	115,702	177,037	5.21%	53,762	204,768	3,570,638
85/84	2047	0	3,570,638	0	0	118,247	178,534	5.21%	56,672	210,723	3,600,024
86/85	2048	0	3,600,024	0	0	120,848	179,776	5.21%	59,549	216,895	3,624,205
87/86	2049	0	3,624,205	0	0	123,507	180,736	5.21%	62,523	223,300	3,642,624
88/87	2050	0	3,642,624	0	0	126,224	181,398	5.21%	65,355	229,922	3,654,970
89/88	2051	0	3,654,970	0	0	129,001	181,733	5.21%	68,290	236,759	3,660,655
90/89	2052	0	3,660,655	0	0	131,839	181,714	5.21%	71,214	243,854	3,659,140

x - denotes shortfall

See Important Disclosure Information section in this Report for explanations of assumptions, limitations, methodologies, and a glossary.

Worksheet Detail - Combined Details

Scenario : What If 1 using Average Return

		Beginning Portfolio Value								Funds Used	
Event or Ages	Year	Earmarked	Fund All Goals	Additions To Assets	Other Additions	Post Retirement Income	Investment Earnings	Investment Return	Taxes	All Goals	Ending Portfolio Value
91/90	2053	0	3,659,140	0	0	134,740	181,323	5.21%	73,920	251,216	3,650,066
John's Plan Ends	2054	0	3,650,066	0	0	137,704	180,533	5.21%	76,599	258,795	3,632,909
-/92	2055	0	3,632,909	0	0	74,140	179,247	5.21%	80,282	201,114	3,604,900
-/93	2056	0	3,604,900	0	0	75,771	177,515	5.21%	82,856	206,634	3,568,696
Sandy's Plan Ends	2057	0	3,568,696	0	0	77,438	175,395	5.21%	84,571	212,300	3,524,659

x - denotes shortfall

See Important Disclosure Information section in this Report for explanations of assumptions, limitations, methodologies, and a glossary.

Worksheet Detail - Combined Details

Scenario : What If 1 using Average Return

Event or Ages	Year	Funds Used						Ending Portfolio Value
		Retirement	Health Care	Travel	New Retirement Home	Car / Truck John	Car / Truck Sandy	
59/58	2021	0	0	0	0	0	0	1,903,302
60/59	2022	0	0	0	0	0	0	2,065,107
61/60	2023	0	0	0	0	0	0	2,236,940
62/61	2024	0	0	0	0	0	21,349	2,397,110
63/62	2025	0	0	0	0	21,819	0	2,568,080
64/63	2026	0	0	0	0	0	0	2,772,640
John & Sandy Retire	2027	108,250	22,894	6,837	341,843	0	0	2,754,033
66/65	2028	110,632	13,261	6,987	0	0	0	2,759,804
67/66	2029	113,066	14,098	7,141	0	0	0	2,804,140
68/67	2030	115,553	15,024	7,298	0	0	0	2,873,170
69/68	2031	118,095	16,042	7,459	0	0	24,862	2,904,739
70/69	2032	120,693	17,149	7,623	0	25,409	0	2,934,074
71/70	2033	123,349	18,341	7,790	0	0	0	2,998,136
72/71	2034	126,062	19,612	7,962	0	0	0	3,062,344
73/72	2035	128,836	20,954	8,137	0	0	0	3,119,939
74/73	2036	131,670	22,364	8,316	0	0	0	3,176,154
75/74	2037	134,567	23,850	8,499	0	0	0	3,230,720
76/75	2038	137,527	25,421	8,686	0	0	28,953	3,253,304
77/76	2039	140,553	27,080	8,877	0	29,590	0	3,271,922
78/77	2040	143,645	28,813	9,072	0	0	0	3,317,579
79/78	2041	146,805	30,623	9,272	0	0	0	3,360,250
80/79	2042	150,035	32,538	0	0	0	0	3,409,370
81/80	2043	153,336	34,553	0	0	0	0	3,455,387
82/81	2044	156,709	36,670	0	0	0	0	3,497,863
83/82	2045	160,157	38,850	0	0	0	0	3,536,430
84/83	2046	163,680	41,088	0	0	0	0	3,570,638
85/84	2047	167,281	43,442	0	0	0	0	3,600,024
86/85	2048	170,961	45,933	0	0	0	0	3,624,205
87/86	2049	174,722	48,578	0	0	0	0	3,642,624
88/87	2050	178,566	51,356	0	0	0	0	3,654,970
89/88	2051	182,495	54,264	0	0	0	0	3,660,655

x - denotes shortfall

See Important Disclosure Information section in this Report for explanations of assumptions, limitations, methodologies, and a glossary.

Worksheet Detail - Combined Details

Scenario : What If 1 using Average Return

Event or Ages	Year	Funds Used: Retirement	Health Care	Travel	New Retirement Home	Car / Truck John	Car / Truck Sandy	Ending Portfolio Value
90/89	2052	186,510	57,345	0	0	0	0	3,659,140
91/90	2053	190,613	60,603	0	0	0	0	3,650,066
John's Plan Ends	2054	194,806	63,988	0	0	0	0	3,632,909
-/92	2055	167,657	33,458	0	0	0	0	3,604,900
-/93	2056	171,345	35,289	0	0	0	0	3,568,696
Sandy's Plan Ends	2057	175,115	37,185	0	0	0	0	3,524,659

Notes

- Calculations are based on a "Rolling Year" rather than a Calendar Year. The current date begins the 365-day "Rolling Year".
- Additions and withdrawals occur at the beginning of the year.
- Other Additions come from items entered in the Other Assets section and any applicable proceeds from insurance policies.
- Stock Options and Restricted Stock values are after-tax.
- Strategy Income is based on the particulars of the Goal Strategies selected. Strategy Income from immediate annuities, 72(t) distributions, and variable annuities with a guaranteed minimum withdrawal benefit (GMWB) is pre-tax. Strategy Income from Net Unrealized Appreciation (NUA) is after-tax.
- Post Retirement Income includes the following: Social Security, pension, annuity, rental property, royalty, alimony, part-time employment, trust, and any other retirement income as entered in the Plan.
- When married, if either Social Security Program Estimate or Use a Better Estimate of Annual Benefits is selected for a participant, the program will default to the greater of the selected benefit or the age adjusted spousal benefit, which is based on the other participant's benefit.
- Investment Earnings are calculated on all assets after any withdrawals for 'Goal Expense', 'Taxes on Withdrawals' and 'Tax Penalties' are subtracted.
- The taxes column is a sum of (1) taxes on retirement income, (2) taxes on strategy income, (3) taxes on withdrawals from qualified assets for Required Minimum Distributions, (4) taxes on withdrawals from taxable assets' untaxed gain used to fund Goals in that year, (5) taxes on withdrawals from tax-deferred or qualified assets used to fund Goals in that year, and (6) taxes on the investment earnings of taxable assets. Tax rates used are detailed in the Tax and Inflation Options page. (Please note, the Taxes column does not include any taxes owed from the exercise of Stock Options or the vesting of Restricted Stock.)
- Tax Penalties can occur when Qualified and Tax-Deferred Assets are used prior to age 59½. If there is a value in this column, it illustrates that you are using your assets in this Plan in a manner that may incur tax penalties. Generally, it is better to avoid tax penalties whenever possible.
- These calculations do not incorporate penalties associated with use of 529 Plan withdrawals for non-qualified expenses.
- Funds for each Goal Expense are first used from Earmarked Assets. If sufficient funds are not available from Earmarked Assets, Fund All Goals Assets will be used to fund the remaining portion of the Goal Expense, if available in that year.
- All funds needed for a Goal must be available in the year the Goal occurs. Funds from Earmarked Assets that become available after the Goal year(s) have passed are not included in the funding of that Goal, and accumulate until the end of the Plan.
- When married, ownership of qualified assets is assumed to roll over to the surviving co-client at the death of the original owner. It is also assumed the surviving co-client inherits all assets of the original owner.

x - denotes shortfall

See Important Disclosure Information section in this Report for explanations of assumptions, limitations, methodologies, and a glossary.

Worksheet Detail - Combined Details

Scenario : What If 1 using Bad Timing

These pages provide a picture of how your Investment Portfolio may hypothetically perform over the life of this Plan. The graph shows the effect on the value of your Investment Portfolio for each year. The chart shows the detailed activities that increase and decrease your Investment Portfolio value each year including the funds needed to pay for each of your Goals. Shortfalls that occur in a particular year are denoted with an 'X' under the Goal column.

Total Portfolio Value Graph

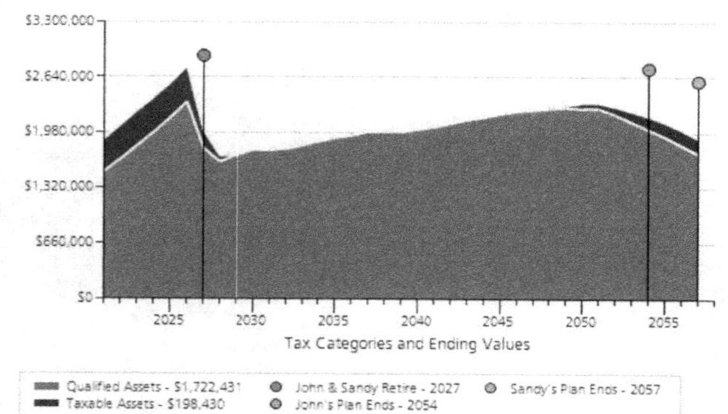

x - denotes shortfall

See Important Disclosure Information section in this Report for explanations of assumptions, limitations, methodologies, and a glossary.

Worksheet Detail - Combined Details

Scenario : What If 1 using Bad Timing

Event or Ages	Year	Beginning Portfolio Value: Earmarked	Beginning Portfolio Value: Fund All Goals	Additions To Assets	Other Additions	Post Retirement Income	Investment Earnings	Investment Return	Taxes	Funds Used: All Goals	Ending Portfolio Value
59/58	2021	0	1,750,000	57,100	0	0	101,433	5.61%	5,231	0	1,903,302
60/59	2022	0	1,903,302	57,212	0	0	110,044	5.61%	5,451	0	2,065,107
61/60	2023	0	2,065,107	58,327	0	0	119,188	5.61%	5,681	0	2,236,940
62/61	2024	0	2,236,940	59,444	0	0	127,698	5.61%	5,623	21,349	2,397,110
63/62	2025	0	2,397,110	61,564	0	0	136,781	5.61%	5,556	21,819	2,568,080
64/63	2026	0	2,568,080	62,686	0	0	147,665	5.61%	5,790	0	2,772,640
John & Sandy Retire	2027	0	2,772,640	0	325,000	0	-620,820	-23.72%	0	479,824	1,996,996
66/65	2028	0	1,996,996	0	0	0	-172,670	-9.25%	0	130,880	1,693,446
67/66	2029	0	1,693,446	0	0	42,105	119,535	7.49%	5,778	134,305	1,715,002
68/67	2030	0	1,715,002	0	0	81,682	122,787	7.49%	19,936	137,875	1,761,660
69/68	2031	0	1,761,660	0	0	83,479	123,562	7.49%	29,469	166,458	1,772,773
70/69	2032	0	1,772,773	0	0	85,315	124,132	7.49%	30,386	170,874	1,780,961
71/70	2033	0	1,780,961	0	0	87,192	127,110	7.49%	22,101	149,480	1,823,682
72/71	2034	0	1,823,682	0	0	89,110	130,084	7.49%	22,896	153,637	1,866,343
73/72	2035	0	1,866,343	0	0	91,071	133,043	7.49%	23,724	157,926	1,908,807
74/73	2036	0	1,908,807	0	0	93,074	135,979	7.49%	24,584	162,350	1,950,926
75/74	2037	0	1,950,926	0	0	95,122	138,879	7.49%	25,479	166,916	1,992,532
76/75	2038	0	1,992,532	0	0	97,215	138,788	7.49%	36,717	200,587	1,991,231
77/76	2039	0	1,991,231	0	0	99,353	138,348	7.49%	37,916	206,100	1,984,917
78/77	2040	0	1,984,917	0	0	101,539	140,593	7.49%	28,391	181,531	2,017,128
79/78	2041	0	2,017,128	0	0	103,773	142,708	7.49%	29,434	186,701	2,047,474
80/79	2042	0	2,047,474	0	0	106,056	145,633	7.49%	27,151	182,573	2,089,440
81/80	2043	0	2,089,440	0	0	108,389	148,475	7.49%	28,210	187,888	2,130,205
82/81	2044	0	2,130,205	0	0	110,774	151,213	7.49%	29,314	193,379	2,169,500
83/82	2045	0	2,169,500	0	0	113,211	153,773	7.49%	31,298	199,007	2,206,179
84/83	2046	0	2,206,179	0	0	115,702	156,123	7.49%	33,425	204,768	2,239,810
85/84	2047	0	2,239,810	0	0	118,247	158,223	7.49%	35,763	210,723	2,269,795
86/85	2048	0	2,269,795	0	0	120,848	160,040	7.49%	38,139	216,895	2,295,649
87/86	2049	0	2,295,649	0	0	123,507	161,525	7.49%	40,683	223,300	2,316,698
88/87	2050	0	2,316,698	0	0	126,224	162,640	7.49%	43,268	229,922	2,332,372
89/88	2051	0	2,332,372	0	0	129,001	163,339	7.49%	45,940	236,759	2,342,013
90/89	2052	0	2,342,013	0	0	131,839	113,726	5.21%	48,235	243,854	2,295,489

x - denotes shortfall

See Important Disclosure Information section in this Report for explanations of assumptions, limitations, methodologies, and a glossary.

Worksheet Detail - Combined Details

Scenario : What If 1 using Bad Timing

		Beginning Portfolio Value								Funds Used	
Event or Ages	Year	Earmarked	Fund All Goals	Additions To Assets	Other Additions	Post Retirement Income	Investment Earnings	Investment Return	Taxes	All Goals	Ending Portfolio Value
91/90	2053	0	2,295,489	0	0	134,740	111,007	5.21%	49,734	251,216	2,240,286
John's Plan Ends	2054	0	2,240,286	0	0	137,704	107,831	5.21%	51,177	258,795	2,175,849
-/92	2055	0	2,175,849	0	0	74,140	104,100	5.21%	52,824	201,114	2,100,150
-/93	2056	0	2,100,150	0	0	75,771	99,899	5.21%	54,081	206,634	2,015,105
Sandy's Plan Ends	2057	0	2,015,105	0	0	77,438	95,241	5.21%	54,623	212,300	1,920,861

x - denotes shortfall

See Important Disclosure Information section in this Report for explanations of assumptions, limitations, methodologies, and a glossary.

Worksheet Detail - Combined Details

Scenario : What If 1 using Bad Timing

Event or Ages	Year	Funds Used						Ending Portfolio Value
		Retirement	Health Care	Travel	New Retirement Home	Car / Truck John	Car / Truck Sandy	
59/58	2021	0	0	0	0	0	0	1,903,302
60/59	2022	0	0	0	0	0	0	2,065,107
61/60	2023	0	0	0	0	0	0	2,236,940
62/61	2024	0	0	0	0	0	21,349	2,397,110
63/62	2025	0	0	0	0	21,819	0	2,568,080
64/63	2026	0	0	0	0	0	0	2,772,640
John & Sandy Retire	2027	108,250	22,894	6,837	341,843	0	0	1,996,996
66/65	2028	110,632	13,261	6,987	0	0	0	1,693,446
67/66	2029	113,066	14,098	7,141	0	0	0	1,715,002
68/67	2030	115,553	15,024	7,298	0	0	0	1,761,660
69/68	2031	118,095	16,042	7,459	0	0	24,862	1,772,773
70/69	2032	120,693	17,149	7,623	0	25,409	0	1,780,961
71/70	2033	123,349	18,341	7,790	0	0	0	1,823,682
72/71	2034	126,062	19,612	7,962	0	0	0	1,866,343
73/72	2035	128,836	20,954	8,137	0	0	0	1,908,807
74/73	2036	131,670	22,364	8,316	0	0	0	1,950,926
75/74	2037	134,567	23,850	8,499	0	0	0	1,992,532
76/75	2038	137,527	25,421	8,686	0	0	28,953	1,991,231
77/76	2039	140,553	27,080	8,877	0	29,590	0	1,984,917
78/77	2040	143,645	28,813	9,072	0	0	0	2,017,128
79/78	2041	146,805	30,623	9,272	0	0	0	2,047,474
80/79	2042	150,035	32,538	0	0	0	0	2,089,440
81/80	2043	153,336	34,553	0	0	0	0	2,130,205
82/81	2044	156,709	36,670	0	0	0	0	2,169,500
83/82	2045	160,157	38,850	0	0	0	0	2,206,179
84/83	2046	163,680	41,088	0	0	0	0	2,239,810
85/84	2047	167,281	43,442	0	0	0	0	2,269,795
86/85	2048	170,961	45,933	0	0	0	0	2,295,649
87/86	2049	174,722	48,578	0	0	0	0	2,316,698
88/87	2050	178,566	51,356	0	0	0	0	2,332,372
89/88	2051	182,495	54,264	0	0	0	0	2,342,013

x - denotes shortfall

See Important Disclosure Information section in this Report for explanations of assumptions, limitations, methodologies, and a glossary.

Worksheet Detail - Combined Details

Scenario : What If 1 using Bad Timing

		Funds Used						
Event or Ages	Year	Retirement	Health Care	Travel	New Retirement Home	Car / Truck John	Car / Truck Sandy	Ending Portfolio Value
90/89	2052	186,510	57,345	0	0	0	0	2,295,489
91/90	2053	190,613	60,603	0	0	0	0	2,240,286
John's Plan Ends	2054	194,806	63,988	0	0	0	0	2,175,849
-/92	2055	167,657	33,458	0	0	0	0	2,100,150
-/93	2056	171,345	35,289	0	0	0	0	2,015,105
Sandy's Plan Ends	2057	175,115	37,185	0	0	0	0	1,920,861

Notes

- Calculations are based on a "Rolling Year" rather than a Calendar Year. The current date begins the 365-day "Rolling Year".
- Additions and withdrawals occur at the beginning of the year.
- Other Additions come from items entered in the Other Assets section and any applicable proceeds from insurance policies.
- Stock Options and Restricted Stock values are after-tax.
- Strategy Income is based on the particulars of the Goal Strategies selected. Strategy Income from immediate annuities, 72(t) distributions, and variable annuities with a guaranteed minimum withdrawal benefit (GMWB) is pre-tax. Strategy Income from Net Unrealized Appreciation (NUA) is after-tax.
- Post Retirement Income includes the following: Social Security, pension, annuity, rental property, royalty, alimony, part-time employment, trust, and any other retirement income as entered in the Plan.
- When married, if either Social Security Program Estimate or Use a Better Estimate of Annual Benefits is selected for a participant, the program will default to the greater of the selected benefit or the age adjusted spousal benefit, which is based on the other participant's benefit.
- Investment Earnings are calculated on all assets after any withdrawals for 'Goal Expense', 'Taxes on Withdrawals' and 'Tax Penalties' are subtracted.
- The taxes column is a sum of (1) taxes on retirement income, (2) taxes on strategy income, (3) taxes on withdrawals from qualified assets for Required Minimum Distributions, (4) taxes on withdrawals from taxable assets' untaxed gain used to fund Goals in that year, (5) taxes on withdrawals from tax-deferred or qualified assets used to fund Goals in that year, and (6) taxes on the investment earnings of taxable assets. Tax rates used are detailed in the Tax and Inflation Options page. (Please note, the Taxes column does not include any taxes owed from the exercise of Stock Options or the vesting of Restricted Stock.)
- Tax Penalties can occur when Qualified and Tax-Deferred Assets are used prior to age 59½. If there is a value in this column, it illustrates that you are using your assets in this Plan in a manner that may incur tax penalties. Generally, it is better to avoid tax penalties whenever possible.
- These calculations do not incorporate penalties associated with use of 529 Plan withdrawals for non-qualified expenses.
- Funds for each Goal Expense are first used from Earmarked Assets. If sufficient funds are not available from Earmarked Assets, Fund All Goals Assets will be used to fund the remaining portion of the Goal Expense, if available in that year.
- All funds needed for a Goal must be available in the year the Goal occurs. Funds from Earmarked Assets that become available after the Goal year(s) have passed are not included in the funding of that Goal, and accumulate until the end of the Plan.
- When married, ownership of qualified assets is assumed to roll over to the surviving co-client at the death of the original owner. It is also assumed the surviving co-client inherits all assets of the original owner.

x - denotes shortfall

See Important Disclosure Information section in this Report for explanations of assumptions, limitations, methodologies, and a glossary.

Worksheet Detail - Social Security Analysis

Social Security Analysis for What If 1

Social Security Strategy	Selected Strategy	As Soon As Possible	At Retirement	At FRA	At Age 70	John begins at age 70 and Sandy begins at FRA
Start age						
John	67	62	65	67	70	70
Sandy	67	62	64	67	70	67
First year benefit in current dollars						
John	$35,377	$0	$30,660	$35,377	$43,868	$43,868
Sandy	$31,776	$0	$25,421	$31,776	$39,402	$31,776
Total lifetime benefit in current dollars	$1,820,339	$1,390,495	$1,662,250	$1,820,339	$2,007,410	$1,934,961
Probability of success	84%	74%	81%	84%	87%	86%
Break Even Point						
John	72	N/A	65	72	76	75
Sandy	71	N/A	64	71	75	74

See Important Disclosure Information section in this Report for explanations of assumptions, limitations, methodologies, and a glossary.

Worksheet Detail - Social Security Analysis

Social Security Analysis for What If 1

Notes

Selected Strategy:

This is the strategy you selected.

At FRA:

You apply for and begin retirement benefits at your Full Retirement Age (FRA), which is determined by your date of birth. If the retirement age you specified is after your FRA, we assume you will begin benefits at FRA, and we will adjust the benefit for inflation until your retirement age.

At Retirement:

You apply for and begin retirement benefits at the retirement age shown. The benefit is automatically adjusted to account for excess earnings from part-time work and/or taking benefits prior to your FRA, if either is applicable.

As soon as possible:

You apply for and begin benefits at the later of your current age or age 62. The benefit is automatically adjusted to account for excess earnings from part-time work, if applicable, and taking benefits prior to your FRA.

At age 70:

You apply for and begin benefits at age 70.

(Higher Wage Earner) begins at age 70 and (Lower Wage Earner) begins at FRA:

This strategy is available only if you are married. The higher wage earner applies for and begins benefits at age 70. The lower wage earner applies for and begins benefits at his/her FRA. The higher/lower wage earners are determined based on the employment incomes you specified.

(Higher Wage Earner) files/suspends and (Lower Wage Earner) restricted application:

This strategy is available only if you are married and assumes that you filed for and suspended your benefits prior to April 30, 2016 and your spouse reached age 62 by January 1, 2016. The higher wage earner applies for and suspends taking benefits until age 70. The higher wage earner can file at or after his/her FRA, at which time the spouse (the lower wage earner) files for and takes spousal benefits. The spouse then files for and begins his/her own benefit at age 70, at the higher benefit amount.

The lower wage earner makes a restricted application at his/her FRA. Restricted application allows the account holder to apply only for the spousal benefit s/he would be due under dual entitlement rules. At any age beyond his/her FRA, the lower wage earner can apply for and receive benefits based on his/her own work history.

After April 30, 2016, you (or your spouse) can still file and suspend your benefits upon reaching your FRA; but this strategy (that allowed your spouse to receive spousal benefits for the same period that the benefits are suspended) has been discontinued by the Social Security Administration.

(Lower Wage Earner) files/suspends and (Higher Wage Earner) restricted application:

This strategy is available only if you are married and assumes that you filed for and suspended your benefits prior to April 30, 2016 and your spouse reached age 62 by January 1, 2016. The lower wage earner applies for and suspends taking benefits until age 70. The lower wage earner can file at or after his/her FRA, at which time the spouse (the higher wage earner) files for and takes spousal benefits. The spouse then files for and begins his/her own benefit at age 70, at the higher benefit amount.

The higher wage earner makes a restricted application at his/her FRA. Restricted application allows the account holder to apply only for the spousal benefit s/he would be due under dual entitlement rules. At any age beyond his/her FRA, the higher wage earner can apply for and receive benefits based on his/her own work history.

After April 30, 2016, you (or your spouse) can still file and suspend your benefits upon reaching your FRA; but this strategy (that allowed your spouse to receive spousal benefits for the same period that the benefits are suspended) has been discontinued by the Social Security Administration.

Maximized Benefits:

This is the strategy that provides the highest estimate of lifetime Social Security income, assuming you live to the age(s) shown on the Detailed Results page.

Total Lifetime Benefit:

The total estimate of benefits you and your co-client, if applicable, would receive in your lifetime, assuming you live to the age(s) shown on the Detailed Results page. This amount is in current (non-inflated) dollars.

Break Even Point:

The age(s) at which this strategy would provide greater benefits than the As Soon As Possible strategy. If you live longer than the break even age for a strategy, your total lifetime benefits using that strategy would be greater than the lifetime benefits of the "As Soon As Possible" strategy. If you are older than age 62, the break even comparison uses the strategy that begins at the earliest age(s) as the baseline for comparison.

See Important Disclosure Information section in this Report for explanations of assumptions, limitations, methodologies, and a glossary.

Worksheet Detail - Social Security Combined Details

Social Security Combined Details for What If 1

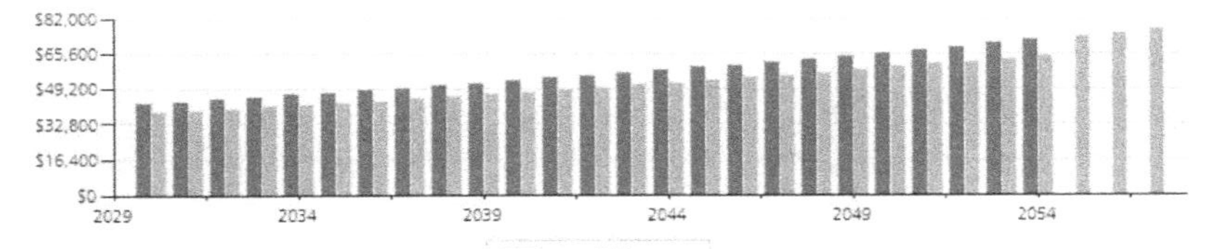

Year	Ages/Event	John	Sandy
2029	67 / 66	$42,105	
2030	68 / 67	$43,031	$38,651
2031	69 / 68	$43,978	$39,501
2032	70 / 69	$44,945	$40,370
2033	71 / 70	$45,934	$41,258
2034	72 / 71	$46,945	$42,166
2035	73 / 72	$47,977	$43,093
2036	74 / 73	$49,033	$44,042
2037	75 / 74	$50,112	$45,010
2038	76 / 75	$51,214	$46,001
2039	77 / 76	$52,341	$47,013
2040	78 / 77	$53,492	$48,047
2041	79 / 78	$54,669	$49,104
2042	80 / 79	$55,872	$50,184
2043	81 / 80	$57,101	$51,288
2044	82 / 81	$58,357	$52,417
2045	83 / 82	$59,641	$53,570

Year	Ages/Event	John	Sandy
2046	84 / 83	$60,953	$54,748
2047	85 / 84	$62,294	$55,953
2048	86 / 85	$63,665	$57,184
2049	87 / 86	$65,065	$58,442
2050	88 / 87	$66,497	$59,728
2051	89 / 88	$67,960	$61,042
2052	90 / 89	$69,455	$62,385
2053	91 / 90	$70,983	$63,757
2054	John's Plan Ends	$72,544	$65,160
2055	- / 92		$74,140
2056	- / 93		$75,771
2057	Sandy's Plan Ends		$77,438

Notes

Assumption for Cost of Living Adjustment (COLA) is 2.20% annually.

See Important Disclosure Information section in this Report for explanations of assumptions, limitations, methodologies, and a glossary.

Worksheet Detail - Health Care Expense Schedule

Scenario : What If 1

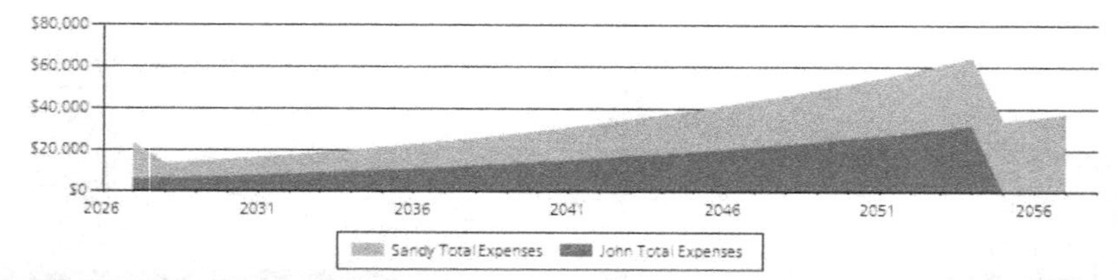

Year	Age/Event	John							Annual Total
		Private Insurance Prior to Medicare	Out-of-Pocket Prior to Medicare	Medicare Part B	Medicare Part D	Medigap Policy	Out-of-Pocket During Medicare	John's Total	
2027	John retires and starts Medicare, Sandy retires	$0	$0	$2,402	$488	$2,077	$1,333	$6,299	$22,894
2028	Sandy starts Medicare	$0	$0	$2,524	$513	$2,242	$1,411	$6,690	$13,261
2029	67/66	$0	$0	$2,653	$539	$2,439	$1,493	$7,124	$14,098
2030	68/67	$0	$0	$2,788	$566	$2,666	$1,580	$7,601	$15,024
2031	69/68	$0	$0	$2,930	$595	$2,926	$1,672	$8,124	$16,042
2032	70/69	$0	$0	$3,080	$626	$3,215	$1,770	$8,690	$17,149
2033	71/70	$0	$0	$3,237	$658	$3,529	$1,873	$9,297	$18,341
2034	72/71	$0	$0	$3,402	$691	$3,866	$1,982	$9,941	$19,612
2035	73/72	$0	$0	$3,576	$726	$4,224	$2,091	$10,616	$20,954
2036	74/73	$0	$0	$3,758	$763	$4,601	$2,206	$11,329	$22,364
2037	75/74	$0	$0	$3,950	$802	$5,002	$2,327	$12,081	$23,850
2038	76/75	$0	$0	$4,151	$843	$5,428	$2,453	$12,875	$25,421

See Important Disclosure Information section in this Report for explanations of assumptions, limitations, methodologies, and a glossary.

Worksheet Detail - Health Care Expense Schedule

Scenario : What If 1

Year	Age/Event	John							Annual Total
		Private Insurance Prior to Medicare	Out-of-Pocket Prior to Medicare	Medicare Part B	Medicare Part D	Medigap Policy	Out-of-Pocket During Medicare	John's Total	
2039	77/76	$0	$0	$4,363	$886	$5,878	$2,588	$13,715	$27,080
2040	78/77	$0	$0	$4,585	$931	$6,350	$2,715	$14,582	$28,813
2041	79/78	$0	$0	$4,819	$979	$6,850	$2,848	$15,496	$30,623
2042	80/79	$0	$0	$5,065	$1,029	$7,381	$2,987	$16,462	$32,538
2043	81/80	$0	$0	$5,323	$1,081	$7,940	$3,131	$17,475	$34,553
2044	82/81	$0	$0	$5,595	$1,137	$8,527	$3,284	$18,542	$36,670
2045	83/82	$0	$0	$5,880	$1,194	$9,143	$3,399	$19,616	$38,850
2046	84/83	$0	$0	$6,180	$1,255	$9,790	$3,520	$20,745	$41,088
2047	85/84	$0	$0	$6,495	$1,319	$10,475	$3,645	$21,934	$43,442
2048	86/85	$0	$0	$6,826	$1,387	$11,212	$3,773	$23,198	$45,933
2049	87/86	$0	$0	$7,174	$1,457	$11,994	$3,909	$24,535	$48,578
2050	88/87	$0	$0	$7,540	$1,532	$12,817	$4,045	$25,934	$51,356
2051	89/88	$0	$0	$7,925	$1,610	$13,671	$4,189	$27,394	$54,264
2052	90/89	$0	$0	$8,329	$1,692	$14,541	$4,403	$28,964	$57,345
2053	91/90	$0	$0	$8,754	$1,778	$15,435	$4,627	$30,594	$60,603
2054	John's plan ends	$0	$0	$9,200	$1,869	$16,356	$4,863	$32,288	$63,988
2055	-/92	$0	$0	$0	$0	$0	$0	$0	$33,458
2056	-/93	$0	$0	$0	$0	$0	$0	$0	$35,289
2057	Sandy's plan ends	$0	$0	$0	$0	$0	$0	$0	$37,185
Total Lifetime Cost of Health Care				**$462,142**					

See Important Disclosure Information section in this Report for explanations of assumptions, limitations, methodologies, and a glossary.

Worksheet Detail - Health Care Expense Schedule

Scenario : What If 1

Year	Age/Event	Sandy							Annual Total
		Private Insurance Prior to Medicare	Out-of-Pocket Prior to Medicare	Medicare Part B	Medicare Part D	Medigap Policy	Out-of-Pocket During Medicare	Sandy's Total	
2027	John retires and starts Medicare, Sandy retires	$11,223	$5,372	$0	$0	$0	$0	$16,595	$22,894
2028	Sandy starts Medicare	$0	$0	$2,524	$513	$2,183	$1,351	$6,571	$13,261
2029	67/66	$0	$0	$2,653	$539	$2,357	$1,426	$6,975	$14,098
2030	68/67	$0	$0	$2,788	$566	$2,563	$1,505	$7,423	$15,024
2031	69/68	$0	$0	$2,930	$595	$2,802	$1,590	$7,918	$16,042
2032	70/69	$0	$0	$3,080	$626	$3,075	$1,678	$8,459	$17,149
2033	71/70	$0	$0	$3,237	$658	$3,379	$1,771	$9,044	$18,341
2034	72/71	$0	$0	$3,402	$691	$3,709	$1,869	$9,672	$19,612
2035	73/72	$0	$0	$3,576	$726	$4,063	$1,972	$10,337	$20,954
2036	74/73	$0	$0	$3,758	$763	$4,439	$2,075	$11,035	$22,364
2037	75/74	$0	$0	$3,950	$802	$4,836	$2,181	$11,769	$23,850
2038	76/75	$0	$0	$4,151	$843	$5,257	$2,294	$12,546	$25,421
2039	77/76	$0	$0	$4,363	$886	$5,704	$2,411	$13,365	$27,080
2040	78/77	$0	$0	$4,585	$931	$6,178	$2,537	$14,232	$28,813
2041	79/78	$0	$0	$4,819	$979	$6,674	$2,656	$15,128	$30,623
2042	80/79	$0	$0	$5,065	$1,029	$7,199	$2,783	$16,076	$32,538
2043	81/80	$0	$0	$5,323	$1,081	$7,758	$2,915	$17,078	$34,553
2044	82/81	$0	$0	$5,595	$1,137	$8,345	$3,052	$18,128	$36,670
2045	83/82	$0	$0	$5,880	$1,194	$8,962	$3,197	$19,234	$38,850
2046	84/83	$0	$0	$6,180	$1,255	$9,610	$3,298	$20,343	$41,088
2047	85/84	$0	$0	$6,495	$1,319	$10,289	$3,404	$21,508	$43,442

See Important Disclosure Information section in this Report for explanations of assumptions, limitations, methodologies, and a glossary.

Worksheet Detail - Health Care Expense Schedule

Scenario : What If 1

Year	Age/Event	Sandy							Annual Total
		Private Insurance Prior to Medicare	Out-of-Pocket Prior to Medicare	Medicare Part B	Medicare Part D	Medigap Policy	Out-of-Pocket During Medicare	Sandy's Total	
2048	86/85	$0	$0	$6,826	$1,387	$11,009	$3,513	$22,735	$45,933
2049	87/86	$0	$0	$7,174	$1,457	$11,784	$3,627	$24,043	$48,578
2050	88/87	$0	$0	$7,540	$1,532	$12,605	$3,745	$25,422	$51,356
2051	89/88	$0	$0	$7,925	$1,610	$13,470	$3,865	$26,870	$54,264
2052	90/89	$0	$0	$8,329	$1,692	$14,368	$3,992	$28,380	$57,345
2053	91/90	$0	$0	$8,754	$1,778	$15,282	$4,195	$30,009	$60,603
2054	John's plan ends	$0	$0	$9,200	$1,869	$16,222	$4,409	$31,700	$63,988
2055	-/92	$0	$0	$9,669	$1,964	$17,190	$4,634	$33,458	$33,458
2056	-/93	$0	$0	$10,163	$2,064	$18,192	$4,870	$35,289	$35,289
2057	Sandy's plan ends	$0	$0	$10,681	$2,170	$19,216	$5,119	$37,185	$37,185
Total Lifetime Cost of Health Care				**$568,525**					

Notes

- Program assumptions:
  - The scenario assumes that client and co-client will each use a combination of Medicare Part A (Hospital Insurance), Part B (Medical Insurance), Part D (Prescription Drug Insurance), Medigap insurance , and Out-of Pocket expenses. Alternatively, Medicare Advantage may be selected instead of Medigap and a Part D plan. The program uses initial default values that may have been adjusted based on your preferences and information provided by you.
  - The scenario assumes that client and co-client each qualify to receive Medicare Part A at no charge and therefore it is not reflected in the Health Care Expense schedule.
  - Medicare and Medigap costs begin at the later of age 65, your retirement age, or the current year.
- All costs are in future dollars.
- Costs associated with Long Term Care needs are not addressed by this goal. A separate LTC goal can be created.
- General Information regarding Medicare:
  - Part B premiums are uniform nationally and are increased for those with a higher Modified Adjusted Gross Income.
  - Part D coverage is optional. Premiums are increased for those with a higher Modified Adjusted Gross Income, differ from state to state, and vary based on the specific plan and level of benefit selected.
  - Medigap coverage is optional and policies (Plans A-N) are issued by private insurers.
  - Clients may incur out-of-pocket healthcare expenses, for costs not covered by Medicare benefits and Medigap insurance.
  - If clients retire before age 65, they may choose to purchase private health insurance or to self-insure. Costs and coverage for private health insurance varies greatly.

See Important Disclosure Information section in this Report for explanations of assumptions, limitations, methodologies, and a glossary.

Glossary

Aspirational Cash Reserve Strategy

This optional strategy simulates setting aside funds to establish an account to fund goals outside of your plan. These funds are segmented out of the investment portfolio and are never spent. Rather, the assets are grown based on the specified investment option and the potential balances are displayed. Generally, this strategy is included when you have excess funds after fulfilling your financial goals and used to create a legacy or to fund discretionary objectives.

Asset Allocation

Asset Allocation is the process of determining what portions of your portfolio holdings are to be invested in the various asset classes.

Asset Class

Asset Class is a standard term that broadly defines a category of investments. The three basic asset classes are Cash, Bonds, and Stocks. Bonds and Stocks are often further subdivided into more narrowly defined classes. Some of the most common asset classes are defined below.

Cash and Cash Alternatives

Cash typically includes bank accounts or certificates of deposit, which are insured by the Federal Deposit Insurance Corporation up to a limit per account. Cash Alternatives typically include money market securities, U.S. treasury bills, and other investments that are readily convertible to cash, have a stable market value, and a very short-term maturity. U.S. Treasury bills are backed by the full faith and credit of the U.S. Government and, when held to maturity, provide safety of principal. (See the "Risks Inherent in Investing" section in this Important Disclosure Information for a summary of the risks associated with investing in cash alternatives.)

Commodities

A commodity is food, metal, or another fixed physical substance that investors buy or sell, usually via futures contracts, and generally traded in very large quantities.

Bonds

Bonds are either domestic (U.S.) or global debt securities issued by either private corporations or governments. (See the "Risks Inherent in Investing" section in this Important Disclosure Information for a summary of the risks associated with investing in bonds. Bonds are also called "fixed income securities.")

Domestic government bonds are backed by the full faith and credit of the U.S. Government and have superior liquidity and, when held to maturity, safety of principal. Domestic corporate bonds carry the credit risk of their issuers and thus usually offer additional yield. Domestic government and corporate bonds can be sub-divided based upon their term to maturity. Short-term bonds have an approximate term to maturity of 1 to 5 years; intermediate-term bonds have an approximate term to maturity of 5 to 10 years; and, long-term bonds have an approximate term to maturity greater than 10 years.

Stocks

Stocks are equity securities of domestic and foreign corporations. (See the "Risks Inherent in Investing" section in this Important Disclosure Information for a summary of the risks associated with investing in stocks.)

Domestic stocks are equity securities of U.S. corporations. Domestic stocks are often sub-divided based upon the market capitalization of the company (the market value of the company's stock). "Large cap" stocks are from larger companies, "mid cap" from the middle range of companies, and "small cap" from smaller, perhaps newer, companies. Generally, small cap stocks experience greater market volatility than stocks of companies with larger capitalization. Small cap stocks are generally those from companies whose capitalization is less than $500 million, mid cap stocks those between $500 million and $5 billion, and large cap over $5 billion.

Large cap, mid cap and small cap may be further sub-divided into "growth" and "value" categories. Growth companies are those with an orientation towards growth, often characterized by commonly used metrics such as higher price-to-book and price-to-earnings ratios. Analogously, value companies are those with an orientation towards value, often characterized by commonly used metrics such as lower price-to-book and price-to-earnings ratios.

International stocks are equity securities from foreign corporations. International stocks are often sub-divided into those from "developed" countries and those from "emerging markets." The emerging markets are in less developed countries with emerging economies that may be characterized by lower income per capita, less developed infrastructure and nascent capital markets. These "emerging markets" usually are less economically and politically stable than the "developed markets." Investing in international stocks involves special risks, among which include foreign exchange volatility and risks of investing under different tax, regulatory and accounting standards.

Glossary

Asset Mix

Asset Mix is the combination of asset classes within a portfolio, and is usually expressed as a percentage for each asset class.

Base Inflation Rate

The Base Inflation Rate is the default inflation rate in the Program. You can adjust this rate in financial goal expenses, retirement income sources, savings rates, and in each What If scenario. Also see "Inflation Rate."

Bear Market Loss

The Bear Market Loss shows how a portfolio would have been impacted during the Great Recession (November 2007 through February 2009) or the Bond Bear Market (July 1979 through February 1980). The Bear Market Loss shows: 1) either the Great Recession Return or the Bond Bear Market Return, whichever is lower, and 2) the potential loss, if you had been invested in this cash-bond-stock-alternative portfolio during the period with the lower return. See Great Recession Return and Bond Bear Market Return.

Bear Market Test

The Bear Market Test, included in the Stress Tests, examines the impact on your Plan results if a Bear Market Loss occurred this year. The Bear Market Test shows the likelihood that you could fund your Needs, Wants and Wishes after experiencing such an event. See Bear Market Loss.

Bond Bear Market Return

The Bond Bear Market Return is the rate of return for a cash-bond-stock-alternative portfolio during the Bond Bear Market (July 1979 through February 1980), the worst bear market for bonds since the Great Depression. Goal Planning & Monitoring shows a Bond Bear Market Return for your Current, Risk-based, and Target Portfolios, calculated using historical returns of four broad-based asset class indices. See Great Recession Return.

Bypass Trust

An estate planning device used to pass down assets after death without subjecting them to the estate tax.

Cash Receipt Schedule

A Cash Receipt Schedule consists of one or more years of future after-tax amounts received from the anticipated sale of an Other Asset, exercising of Stock Options grants, or proceeds from Restricted Stock grants.

Composite Portfolio

The Composite Portfolio provides an aggregated view of your Target Portfolio along with any assets that are considered to be unavailable for reallocation.

Concentrated Position

A Concentrated Position is when your portfolio contains a significant amount (as a percentage of the total portfolio value) in individual stock or bonds. Concentrated Positions have the potential to increase the risk of your portfolio.

Confidence Zone

See Monte Carlo Confidence Zone.

Current Dollars

The Results of Goal Planning & Monitoring calculations are in Future Dollars. To help you compare dollar amounts in different years, we also express the Results in Current Dollars, calculated by discounting the Future Dollars by the sequence of inflation rates used in the Plan.

Current Portfolio

Your Current Portfolio is comprised of all the investment assets you currently own (or a subset of your assets, based on the information you provided for this Plan), categorized by Asset Class and Asset Mix.

Fund All Goals

Fund All Goals is one of two ways for your assets and retirement income to be used to fund your goals. The other is Earmark, which means that an asset or retirement income is assigned to one or more goals, and will be used only for those goals. Fund All Goals means that the asset or income is not earmarked to fund specific goals, and can be used to fund any goal, as needed in the calculations.

Future Dollars

Future Dollars are inflated dollars. The Results of Goal Planning & Monitoring calculations are in Future Dollars. To help you compare dollar amounts in different years, we discount the Future Dollar amounts by the inflation rates used in the calculations and display the Results in the equivalent Current Dollars.

Glossary

Great Recession Return

The Great Recession Return is the rate of return for a cash-bond-stock-alternative portfolio during the Great Recession (November 2007 through February 2009), the worst bear market for stocks since the Great Depression. Goal Planning & Monitoring shows a Great Recession Return for your Current, Risk-based, and Target Portfolios, calculated using historical returns of four broad-based asset class indices. See Bond Bear Market Return.

Inflation Rate

Inflation is the percentage increase in the cost of goods and services for a specified time period. A historical measure of inflation is the Consumer Price Index (CPI). In Goal Planning & Monitoring, the Inflation Rate is selected by your advisor, and can be adjusted in different scenarios.

Irrevocable Life Insurance Trust

An irrevocable trust set up with a life insurance policy as the asset, allowing the grantor of the policy to exempt the asset away from his or her taxable estate.

Liquidity

Liquidity is the ease with which an investment can be converted into cash.

Locked Asset

An asset is considered to be locked by the software if it is unavailable to be reallocated to the Target Portfolio. Any account that has been indicated as locked, as well as specific account types such as Variable Annuity with a Guaranteed Minimum Withdrawal Benefit are considered locked.

Model Portfolio Table

The Model Portfolio Table is the portfolio(s) that could be appropriate for you, based upon the risk-based portfolio.

Monte Carlo Confidence Zone

The Monte Carlo Confidence Zone is the range of probabilities that you (and/or your advisor) have selected as your target range for the Monte Carlo Probability of Success in your Plan. The Confidence Zone reflects the Monte Carlo Probabilities of Success with which you would be comfortable, based upon your Plan, your specific time horizon, risk profile, and other factors unique to you.

Monte Carlo Probability of Success / Probability of Failure

The Monte Carlo Probability of Success is the percentage of trials of your Plan that were successful. If a Monte Carlo simulation runs your Plan 1,000 times, and if 600 of those runs are successful (i.e., all your goals are funded and you have at least $1 of Safety Margin), then the Probability of Success for that Plan, with all its underlying assumptions, would be 60%, and the Probability of Failure would be 40%.

Monte Carlo Simulations

Monte Carlo simulations are used to show how variations in rates of return each year can affect your results. A Monte Carlo simulation calculates the results of your Plan by running it many times, each time using a different sequence of returns. Some sequences of returns will give you better results, and some will give you worse results. These multiple trials provide a range of possible results, some successful (you would have met all your goals) and some unsuccessful (you would not have met all your goals).

Needs / Wants / Wishes

In Goal Planning & Monitoring, you choose an importance level from 10 to 1 (where 10 is the highest) for each of your financial goals. Then, the importance levels are divided into three groups: Needs, Wants, and Wishes. Needs are the goals that you consider necessary for your lifestyle, and are the goals that you must fulfill. Wants are the goals that you would really like to fulfill, but could live without. Wishes are the "dream goals" that you would like to fund, although you won't be too dissatisfied if you can't fund them. In Goal Planning & Monitoring, Needs are your most important goals, then Wants, then Wishes.

Portfolio Set

A Portfolio Set is a group of portfolios that provides a range of risk and return strategies for different investors.

Portfolio Total Return

A Portfolio Total Return is determined by weighting the return assumption for each Asset Class according to the Asset Mix.

Probability of Success / Probability of Failure

See Monte Carlo Probability of Success / Probability of Failure.

Real Return

The Real Return is the Total Return of your portfolio minus the Inflation Rate.

Glossary

Recommended Scenario

The Recommended Scenario is the scenario selected by your advisor to be shown on the Results page and in Play Zone.

Retirement Cash Reserve Strategy

This optional strategy simulates creating a cash account to provide funding for near-term goal expenses. You select the number of years of Needs, Wants, and Wishes to be included in the cash account. The Program then funds the Retirement Cash Reserve with the designated amounts, and simulates rebalancing your remaining investments to match the selected Target Portfolio.

Retirement Start Date

For married couples, retirement in Goal Planning & Monitoring begins when both the client and spouse are retired. For single, divorced, or widowed clients, retirement begins when the client retires.

Risk

Risk is the chance that the actual return of an investment, asset class, or portfolio will be different from its expected or average return.

Risk-based Portfolio

The risk-based portfolio is the Model Portfolio associated with the risk score you selected.

Safety Margin

The Safety Margin is the hypothetical portfolio value at the end of the Plan. A Safety Margin of zero indicates the portfolio was depleted before the Plan ended.

Standard Deviation

Standard Deviation is a statistical measure of the volatility of an investment, an asset class, or a portfolio. It measures the degree by which an actual return might vary from the average return, or mean. Typically, the higher the standard deviation, the higher the potential risk of the investment, asset class, or portfolio.

Star Track

Star Track provides a summary of your Plan results over time, using a bar graph. Each bar shows the Monte Carlo Probability of Success for your Recommended Scenario, on the date specified, compared to the Monte Carlo Probability of Success for a scenario using all Target values.

Target Band

The Target Band is the portfolio(s) that could be appropriate for you, based upon the risk-based portfolio.

Target Goal Amount

The Target Goal Amount is the amount you would expect to spend, or the amount you would like to spend, for each financial goal.

Target Portfolio

Target Portfolio is the portfolio you have selected based upon your financial goals and your risk tolerance.

Target Retirement Age

Target Retirement Age is the age at which you would like to retire.

Target Savings Amount

In the Resources section of Goal Planning & Monitoring, you enter the current annual additions being made to your investment assets. The total of these additions is your Target Savings Amount.

Time Horizon

Time Horizon is the period from now until the time the assets in this portfolio will begin to be used.

Total Return

Total Return is an assumed, hypothetical growth rate for a specified time period. The Total Return is either (1) the Portfolio Total Return or (2) as entered by you or your advisor. Also see "Real Return."

Wants

See "Needs / Wants / Wishes".

Willingness

In Goal Planning & Monitoring, in addition to specifying Target Goal Amounts, a Target Savings Amount, and Target Retirement Ages, you also specify a Willingness to adjust these Target values. The Willingness choices are Very Willing, Somewhat Willing, Slightly Willing, and Not at All.

Wishes

See "Needs / Wants / Wishes".

Plan Delivery Acknowledgement

This Plan should be reviewed periodically to ensure that the decisions made continue to be appropriate, particularly if there are changes in family circumstances including, but not limited to an inheritance, birth of a child, death of a family member, or material change in incomes or expenses.

We (John and Sandy Grey) have reviewed and accept the information contained within this Plan and understand the assumptions associated with it. We believe that all information provided by us is complete and accurate to the best of our knowledge. We recognize that performance is not guaranteed and that all future projections are included simply as a tool for decision making and do not represent a forecast of our financial future.

Your advisor (Mark Aho) will review this Plan with you on a periodic basis to determine whether your stated goals and assumptions in this Plan are still relevant. It is not expected that the Plan will change frequently. In particular, short-term changes in the financial markets should not generally require adjustments to the Plan. It is your obligation to notify all interested parties of any material changes that would alter the objectives of this Plan. If all interested parties are not notified of any material changes, then the current Plan document would become invalid.

Client signature & date

Advisor signature & date

Delivery Date

Notes

We have prepared this Plan based on information provided by you. We have not attempted to verify the accuracy or completeness of this information. As the future cannot be forecast with certainty, actual results will vary from these projections. It is possible that these variations may be material. The degree of uncertainty normally increases with the length of the future period covered.

APPENDIX C

SAMPLE PERSONAL FINANCIAL POLICY STATEMENT

Mark A. Aho, MBA, CFP®,
CIMA®
(906)226-0880
Markahofinancial.com

PERSONAL FINANCIAL POLICY STATEMENT

For
JOHN AND SANDY GREY

Introduction

The **Personal Financial Policy Statement** (PFPS) and Goal Plan are important **written** documents that clearly defines your financial **goals** and **objectives** over a relevant, explicitly stated time horizon. As your financial advisor, **creating** and **maintaining** these documents for you is one of my key responsibilities.

The PFPS and Goal Plan is the foundation of the financial planning process. It establishes a long-term plan which will guide your financial decisions. The Policy Statement and Goal Plan helps to balance your goals and objectives with other essentials. It addresses concerns including: your safety net, debt management, tax planning, educational planning, retirement planning, estate planning, and investment strategy. The PFPS and Goal Plan is designed to help you with your personal financial planning process.

By using a well-constructed PFPS and Goal Plan, you will follow a carefully considered and disciplined approach to financial planning. Many people – and their financial advisors – are tempted to make ad hoc decisions about their financial situation – decisions that are often based on panic or overconfidence. The PFPS and Goal Plan will make sure that you consider the long-term and evolutionary nature of the financial planning process. It will clearly and concisely identify the constraints and opportunities of your current financial situation, while also focusing on your goals and objectives. As a result, your financial plan will attend to your short-term needs without losing sight of your long-term goals. Using the PFPS and Goal Plan, we can work together to establish guidelines that we both feel are appropriate to your situation, given the strategies available and the realities of the marketplace.

It is your responsibility to make sure that the data and information used to construct both the PFPS and Goal Plan is correct. This is your plan, however we will guide you through this process. Once you have established your PFPS and Goal Plan we will help you follow that policy and plan. We will regularly reevaluate and update the PFPS and the Goal Plan. The PFPS and Goal Plan will most likely evolve in response to personal and family changes, and the overall capital market conditions. Both the PFPS and Goal Plan must adapt to these changes.

A professionally prepared PFPS and Goal Plan will track your progress, and it will provide continuity from one year to the next. The PFPS and Goal Plan will also help to prevent misunderstandings, because it clearly explains the nature of our relationship and the strategies we have agreed to implement. Finally, the PFPS will coordinate the efforts of other professionals (for example: accountants, lawyers) that we choose to consult as part of the financial planning process.

To Summarize: The key elements to reaching your financial objectives and goals are:

1. Believe in the future
2. Making a plan (PFPS and Goal Plan).
3. Staying on that plan (Patience)
4. Asset allocation designed to meet your goals.
5. Disciplined diversification within the selected asset classes.
6. Regular rebalancing, generally annually.

And above all, the year-in, year-out behavioral coaching, which is my ultimate value.

JOHN AND SANDY GREY Advisory Support Team

Financial Advisor: Mark A. Aho 906-226-0880
Relationship Manager: Sally Brown
CPA: Mary Beth Stone
Attorney: Frank Jones

Family Members

Name
1. Sarah, daughter
2. Philip, son
3.
4.

Important other Relationships

Value/Goals and Personal Objectives

1. Retire in the Upper Peninsula
2. Build their dream home
3. Enjoy travel and vacations during retirement
4.

Interests

1. They both enjoy reading
2. Hiking throughout areas of the UP
3. Travel
4. John enjoys golf, and Sandy likes to run outside and cross country ski in the winter

STATEMENT OF INVESTMENT POLICY OBJECTIVES & GUIDELINES

Primary Financial Values and Goals Purpose of the Investment Portfolio

Overall Purpose: The purpose of the portfolio is to build funds for retirement and also a legacy pool of investments for our heirs and favorite charities. During our retirement years it is our goal to obtain income from the portfolio and to increase the income on an annual basis at or above the rate of inflation. At our death it is our goal to have a worthy legacy amount for our heirs and our favorite charities.

Investment Objectives

In order to meet its needs, the investment strategy of JOHN AND SANDY GREY is to emphasize total return: that is, the aggregate return from capital appreciation and dividend and interest income. Specifically, the primary objective in the investment management for investment account assets shall be: **Balanced/Growth:** The primary objective is capital appreciation with some income through investment in equity and fixed income instruments. This overall portfolio will consist primarily of large capitalization and small capitalization equity issues (U.S, developed international, emerging markets will be represented most of the time); May also be invested in alternative investments; will also be invested in fixed income; will be diversified in both sector and security; may experience moderate losses through a market cycle.

Investment Time Horizon

The Investment Time Horizon is the amount of time from today during which it is expected that the majority of the investable assets will remain in this portfolio. If a substantial portion of the portfolio were expected to be liquidated, the investment time horizon would be the number of years until that event. Because JOHN AND SANDY GREY investment portfolio represents a long-term time commitment for future use of the total return from these investments, the investment time horizon is 10+years.

Planned Deposits to Investments

There are no planned deposits at this time.

Need for Liquidity

There is no specific liquidity need at this time.

Need for Income

There is no need for income from this portfolio at this time.

Risk Tolerance

Risk tolerance can best be described as moderate. Willing to accept some risk for an average return on investments. Subject to ongoing monitoring and periodic review, interim fluctuations in market value and rates of return may be tolerated in order to achieve longer-term objectives

Performance Expectations

The long term expectations for investment portfolio return will be measured on a total return basis. The total expected average return is: See goal plan

Performance Review and Evaluation

Total performance relative to objectives and individual manager performance will be reviewed Semi-annually, and evaluated relative to objectives over a 3-5 year market cycle. Investment managers shall be reviewed regarding performance, personnel, strategy, research capabilities, organizational and business matters, and other qualitative factors that may impact their ability to achieve the desired investment results.

Tax Bracket

JOHN AND SANDY GREY currently file a joint tax return and are currently in the 22% marginal Federal income tax bracket

Investment Portfolio Asset Allocation Overview

Asset Class	Minimum	Preferred	Maximum
Cash	1%	1%	20%
Bonds	10%	29%	50%
Stocks	50%	70%	90%

*Generally, no more than a 10% deviation from the preferred allocation is targeted.

Tax Deferred 401K/IRAs

Strategic Asset Allocation by Asset Class

Asset Class	Preferred Exposure	
U.S. Large Cap Growth Stocks	13%	
U.S. Large Cap Value Stocks	13%	
U.S. Small Cap Growth Stocks	13%	
U.S. Small Cap Value Stocks	13%	
Dev. International/Emerging Mkts*	15%	
Global Real Estate-REIT	3%	
U.S. Government/Corporate Bonds	18%	Short-Intermediate Duration/High Quality
Global Bonds	11%	
Cash	1%	
Total	100%	

*Assigned manager will determine allocation towards Developed International and Emerging Market, and monitored internally by MAFG.

Taxable Investment Portfolio

Strategic Asset Allocation by Asset Class

Asset Class	Preferred Exposure	
U.S. Large Capitalization Stocks*	50%	
U.S. Fixed Income Municipal Tax Free	30%	Short-Intermediate Duration/High Quality
U.S. Small Cap Growth	5%	
U.S. Small Cap Value	5%	
Dev. International/Emerging Mkts	10%	
Total	100%	

The portfolio will primarily consist of high quality U.S. large capitalization companies with a global reach. This portfolio is managed on the basis of companies paying and growing their dividends paid to investors. The intent is to have a well-diversified portfolio of at least 25 companies in at least 5 of the 10 S&P sectors. The overall intent of this portfolio is to be invested in high quality companies paying a current and consistently growing dividend.

Rebalancing to Desired Strategy

From time to time, market conditions will cause your portfolio's investments to vary from the original allocation we established. To remain consistent with the overall guidelines established in this Investment Policy statement, each security in which the portfolio is invested may be reviewed at interval, and rebalanced back to the normal weighting.

The financial representative will determine the review interval and the amount of variance allowed in an attempt to balance the goals of proper allocation vs. minimizing transaction costs and fees.

Financial Assets Currently Held at Raymond James

Date	Total Assets
7/13/20201	**1,750,000**

The aggregate fee on your accounts is(are): .96 bps

Financial Assets Retirement/Wealth Building Plan

See Goal Plan.

Estate Planning

Will completed and reviewed on	March, 2018
Executor is	themselves
Power of Attorney	Sarah
Power of Health	Philip
Trust completed and reviewed on	March, 2018
Successor Trustee	Sarah
Long-Term Care	yes – purchased a 10 year payment policy with Nationwide
Umbrella Coverage	yes - $3 million with their insurance agent
Disability Coverage	no

Executor/Trustee Issues

Gifting

No gifting is in the foreseeable future. This will be revisited.

Business Succession Plans Issues

Duties and Responsibilities

The financial representative is responsible to assist the investor in making an appropriate asset allocation decision based on the particular needs, objectives and risk tolerance of the investor. The financial representative will be available on a regular basis to meet with the investor and review the portfolio based on information provided by the investor.

The investor is responsible to provide the financial representative with all relevant and accurate information on financial condition, net worth and risk tolerances and must promptly notify the advisor of any changes to this information.

Recommendations

All of our recommendations will be made in conjunction with this PFPS and Goal Plan. This will ensure that the strategies we choose will be consistent with your goals, objectives and priorities. At times we may make recommendations that we feel are essential to your family's well-being and security, even though these recommendations may not be directly related to issues we have discussed. Nonetheless, all of our recommendations will follow directly from this document, and will be in your best interest.

Our Service - Updates and Reviews

Personal Meetings- Comprehensive Semi Annual Review

Process – How involved do you like to be in managing your finances?

Preferred method of contact - Email/Phone/Letter

Phone Calls-

Basically on an on needed basis by the advisor or the client, however, the advisor service team may call you in the quarter which there was no personal review meeting. We will be available at your convenience and we will make every effort possible to return all messages within 24 hours. We expect the same consideration from you.

Reporting-

Investment Statements Monthly or Quarterly by Account type
Performance Reports: Quarterly by account type
Tax reporting: Annually
PFPS updates: Annually or as required
Goal Plan updates: Semi-Annual Review

Publications- Newsletter: Quarterly

Website and advisor access- markahofinancial.com

Investment Policy Review

Your Financial Advisor will review this Investment Policy Statement (IPS) and your Goal Plan with you at least annually to determine whether stated investment objectives are still relevant. It is not expected that the IPS will change frequently. In particular, short-term changes in the financial markets should not require adjustments to the IPS. It is the obligation of the Client to notify all interested parties of any material changes that would alter the objectives or construction of this portfolio. If all interested parties are not notified of these material changes, then the current investment policy is invalid.
This IPS is not a contractual agreement of any kind and therefore by signing it you will not be bound to any arrangement. It is only meant to be a summary of the agreed upon investment management techniques.

Investing involves risk and you may incur a profit or loss regardless of strategy selected.
Diversification and asset allocation do not ensure a profit or protect against a loss. Dividends are not guaranteed and must be authorized by the company's board of directors. There are special risks associated with investing in bonds such as interest rate risk, market risk, call risk, prepayment risk, credit risk, and reinvestment risk. Small-Cap Stocks: Small-capitalization investing typically carries more risk than investing in well-established "bluechip" companies. Historically, small-cap companies' stock has experienced a greater degree of market volatility than the average stock. Foreign Investing: Changes in currency exchange rates and differences in accounting and taxation policies outside the U.S. can raise or lower returns in foreign investments. Also, some overseas markets may not be as politically and economically stable as the United States and other nations. Emerging Markets: The small size of securities markets in emerging markets and the low trading volume may lead to a lack of liquidity, which leads to increased volatility. Also, emerging markets may not provide adequate legal protection for private or foreign investment or private property. Be advised that investments in real estate and in REITs have various risks, including possible lack of liquidity and devaluation based on adverse economic and regulatory changes. Additionally, investments in REIT's will fluctuate with the value of the underlying properties, and the price at redemption may be more or less than the original price paid. Alternative investments involve substantial risks that may be greater than those associated with traditional investments and may be offered only to clients who meet specific suitability requirements, including minimum net worth tests. Theses risks include but are not limited to: limited or no liquidity, tax considerations, incentive fee structures, speculative investment strategies, and different regulatory and reporting requirements.

Rebalancing a non-retirement account could be a taxable event that may increase your tax liability. In a fee-based account clients pay a quarterly fee, based on the level of assets in the account, for the services of a financial advisor as part of an advisory relationship. In deciding to pay a fee rather than commissions, clients should understand that the fee may be higher than a commission alternative during periods of lower trading. Advisory fees are in addition to the internal expenses charged by mutual funds and other investment company securities. To the extent that clients intend to hold these securities, the internal expenses should be included when evaluating the costs of a fee-based account. Clients should periodically re-evaluate whether the use of an asset-based fee continues to be appropriate in servicing their needs. A list of additional considerations, as well as the fee schedule, is available in the firm's Form ADV Part 2A as well as the client agreement. Past performance does not guarantee future results. Please note that the strategies provided above are general and investment decisions should only be made after a discussion with the appropriate professional about your individual situation. There can be no assurance that any investment will meet its performance objectives or that substantial losses will be avoided. Raymond James does not provide tax or legal services. Please discuss these matters with the appropriate professional.

Mark Aho, CFP®, CIMA®
President, MAFG
Financial Advisors, RJFS

Mark Aho Financial Group
205 N. Lakeshore Blvd., Ste B // Marquette, MI 49855
(906) 226-0880

APPENDIX D

SIX PRINCIPLES OF INVESTING

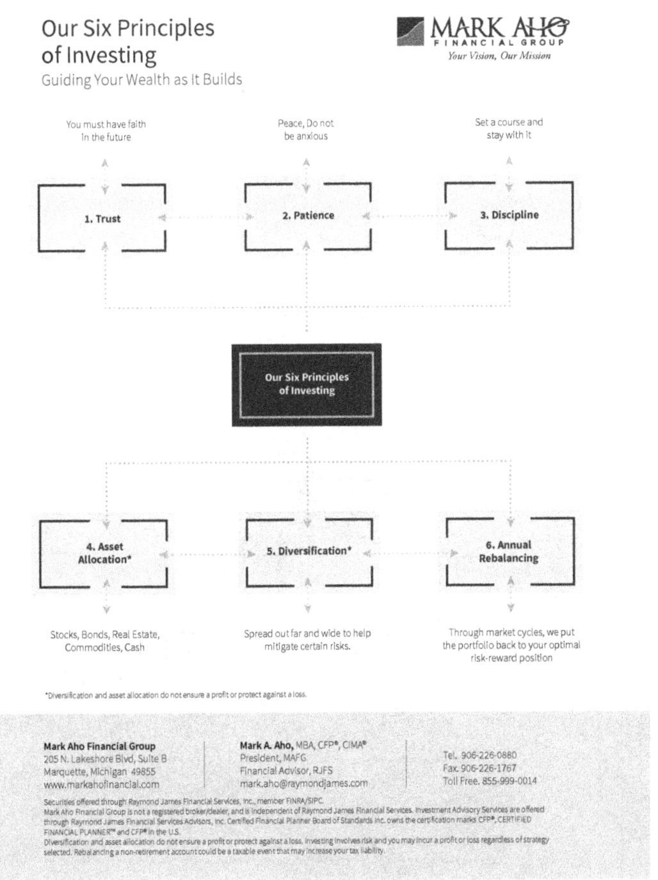

APPENDIX E

START YOUR JOURNEY

Our Advisor's Wealth Management Consultative Process

Define and Follow a Clear Process

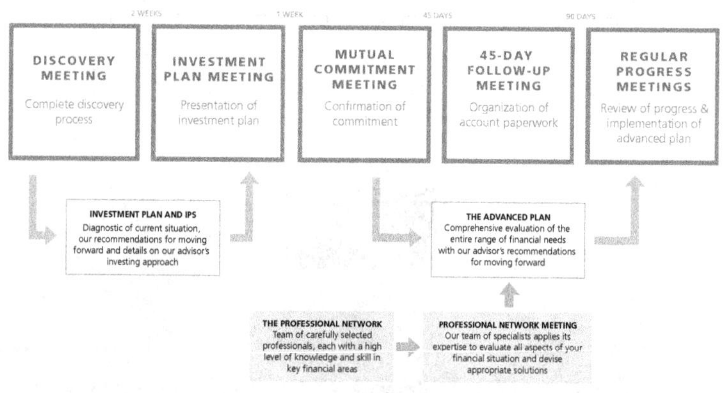

Mark Aho Financial Group
205 N. Lakeshore Blvd, Suite B
Marquette, Michigan 49855
www.markahofinancial.com

Mark A. Aho, MBA, CFP®, CIMA®
President, MAFG
Financial Advisor, RJFS
mark.aho@raymondjames.com

Tel. 906-226-0880
Fax. 906-226-1767
Toll Free. 855-999-0014

Our Advisor's Wealth Management Formula

Investing involves risk and you may incur a profit or loss regardless of strategy selected.

Mark Aho Financial Group
205 N. Lakeshore Blvd, Suite B
Marquette, Michigan 49855
www.markahofinancial.com

Mark A. Aho, MBA, CFP®, CIMA®
President, MAFG
Financial Advisor, RJFS
mark.aho@raymondjames.com

Tel. 906-226-0880
Fax. 906-226-1767
Toll Free. 855-999-0014

Securities offered through Raymond James Financial Services, Inc., member FINRA/SIPC.
Mark Aho Financial Group is not a registered broker/dealer, and is independent of Raymond James Financial Services. Investment Advisory Services are offered through Raymond James Financial Services Advisors, Inc.

APPENDIX F

WHAT TO BRING TO A MEETING WITH YOUR FINANCIAL ADVISOR

- ☐ Income Information: Most recent pay stubs or recent W-2 or 1099. This details your income and deductions or expenses.

- ☐ Current Bank Statements: Checking, savings, and money market accounts.

- ☐ Current Investment Statements: Brokerage accounts, mutual funds, stocks, retirement plans, etc. This information will allow us to analyze your investments and make certain that they match your goals and risk tolerance.

- ☐ Recent Tax Returns: Tax return with all schedules and/or statements. Your income tax return helps us determine your tax efficiency.

- ☐ Loan Information: Mortgages, student loans, credit cards, etc. We need to know about any outstanding debt/loans so we can discuss payoff or payments.

- ☐ List of Assets: Any other items of value which are not included on account statements.

- ☐ Spending Information: Quickbooks reports, Mint.com screen prints, American Express statements, back of the envelope numbers…however you chose to track your expenses. How you spend your money tells us what you really value.

- ☐ Estate Documents: Wills, trusts, powers of attorney. Any estate documents that you have had drawn up.

- ☐ Life Insurance and Disability: Policies or recent statements. We will review amounts and terms of policies.

- ☐ Property and Casualty Insurance: Declaration pages for your home, auto, boat, jewelry, umbrella, and any other policies on your things.

ENDNOTES

CHAPTER 2

1 Covey, Stephen R. *The 7 Habits of Highly Effective People: Powerful Lessons in Personal Change.* (p. 273). New York: RosettaBooks LLC, 2013. Kindle Edition.

2 Covey, Stephen R. *The 7 Habits of Highly Effective People: Powerful Lessons in Personal Change* (p. 272). New York: RosettaBooks LLC, 2013. Kindle Edition

3 Carol S. Dweck, *Mindset: The New Psychology of Success, Updated.* (New York: Ballantine Books, an imprint and division of Penguin Random House, LLC, 2016), 48.

4 https://www.merriam-webster.com/dictionary/investor#other-words Accessed 9.5.20

CHAPTER 4

1 https://winstonchurchill.org/resources/quotes/the-worst-form-of-government/ Accessed 6.15.20

CHAPTER 6

1 https://www.investopedia.com/articles/personal-finance/091615/how-use-your-hsa-retirement.asp. Accessed 10.3.21

CHAPTER 7

1 Chirputkar, Smita. "A Fundamental Look at S&P 500 Dividend Aristocrats," *S&P Dow June Indices*. February 2019. https://us.spindices.com/indexology/dividends/a-fundamental-look-at-sp-500-dividend-aristocrats. Accessed June 2020.

2 https://www.investopedia.com/terms/e/etf.asp Accessed 10.24.21

CHAPTER 8

1 https://www.ssa.gov/pubs/EN-05-10147.pdf

2 https://www.aarp.org/retirement/social-security/questions-answers/medical-conditions/. Accessed 9.15.21

3 https://www.aarp.org. Accessed 4.28.21

4 https://www.aarp.org/retirement/social-security/questions-answers/work-length-social-security.html Accessed 9.27.21

5 https://www.ssa.gov/pubs/EN-05-10072.pdf. Accessed 9.27.21

6 https://www.medicare.gov/what-medicare-covers/your-medicare-coverage-choices. Accessed 8.10.21

CHAPTER 9

1 https://www.irs.gov/retirement-plans/401k-plans. Accessed 9.27.21

2 https://www.irs.gov/retirement-plans/irc-403b-tax-sheltered-annuity-plans Accessed 9.27.21

CHAPTER 10

1 https://www.compassion.com/poverty/opposite-of-poverty.htm accessed 9.24.21

2 https://howmuch.net/articles/distribution-worlds-wealth-2019. Accessed 11/21/20

CHAPTER 11

1 https://www.investopedia.com/articles/markets-economy/090116/what-silver-certificate-dollar-bill-worth-today.asp accessed July 30, 2021

2 https://www.investopedia.com/ask/answers/09/gold-standard.asp Article dated April 27, 2021. Accessed August 8, 2021

3 https://www.investopedia.com/terms/f/fiatmoney.asp. Accessed 9.27.21

CHAPTER 12

1 https://www.imdb.com/title/tt0482629/ Accessed 3.25.21

2 https://www.biblegateway.com/passage/?search=2+Corinthians+9%3A7&version=NLT Accessed 7.30.21

CHAPTER 13

1 https://www.irs.gov/retirement-plans/retirement-plans-faqs-regarding-iras-distributions-withdrawals accessed 7.30.21

ACKNOWLEDGMENTS

Thank you, reader, for allowing me to share a story and the concept of being a family steward. It is my desire to help more and more people become successful family stewards. If you take what you've read here and apply these principles, you and your family will change your legacy forever.

Thank you to my associates in my office who help all of our clients reach their family stewardship goals. Their hard work, dedication, and unending loyalty allow me to devote the time to my other endeavors.

Thank you, Kirsten D. Samuel, for being a wonderful person to work with to complete this book. Your gentle and kind spirit and publishing skills were much appreciated.

Thank you, my clients, for the privilege of helping you achieve your financial and wealth-building goals. Each of you enriches my life.

Most of all, thank you, God the Father and Jesus Christ, the Son, for giving me the faith to forge an unbreakable bond with you.

ABOUT MARK A. AHO

Mark A. Aho is a devoted husband, a dedicated father, and a successful financial advisor in the Upper Peninsula of Michigan. Blessed to be adopted as an infant and raised by loving parents, he embraces the noble notions of faith and family. As a lifelong learner, Mark champions a positive view of the future and anyone's ability to build wealth. Over the years, he has built a team of professionals who reflect his persistent drive for excellence. Mark's passion overflows as he mentors his team and others to serve every client through premium wealth management services.

Mark fully enjoys life by immersing himself in the continual improvement of mind, body, and spirit. He enjoys a lifelong passion for downhill skiing, especially being on a mountain top with breathtaking views around him. Mark also plays golf with friends and clients; however, he finds it to be a most humbling sport that reminds him on every round there is something new to learn each day.

Mark and his wife, Julie, share life together with their two adult children, Christina and Ross.

CONNECT WITH MARK TODAY

Facebook.com/MarkAhoFinancialGroup

LinkedIn.com/in/MarkAho

twitter.com/MarkAhoFinGroup

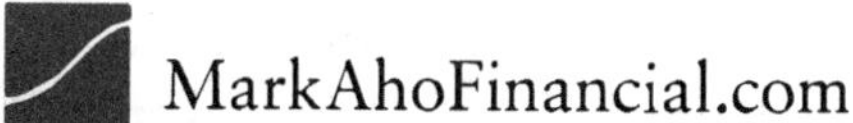
MarkAhoFinancial.com

906-226-0880

Here to help you build and preserve wealth, so you can live abundantly and generously as we help you answer four important questions:

- **Will my family and I be okay?**
- **Will my family and I be able to live the life we want?**
- **Can I be generous to others?**
- **Have I done enough?**

Mark A. Aho Practices Building a Legacy Through Generous Giving to His Favorite Charities

St. Peter Cathedral,
Marquette, Michigan

StPeterCathedral.org

The passion of Bay Cliff will always be children, and the emphasis continues to be on helping those with special needs do the things all children like to do, such as riding a bike, playing games, or taking care of their own personal hygiene.

BayCliff.org

Our mission is to give emotional, spiritual, and material assistance to any woman facing a pregnancy. We are here for those women who have a negative pregnancy test and are at risk for a future unexpected pregnancy, all at no charge.

CareClinicMqt.org

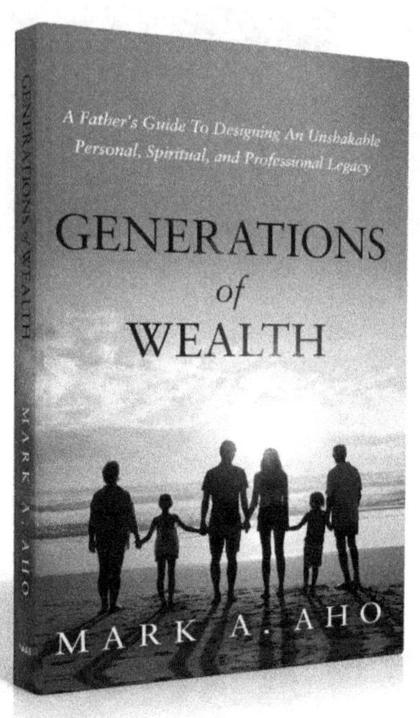
A Father's Guide To Designing An Unshakable
Personal, Spiritual, and Professional Legacy
GENERATIONS
of
WEALTH
MARK A. AHO

CPSIA information can be obtained
at www.ICGtesting.com
Printed in the USA
LVHW080756210322
713963LV00006B/116/J